CONTENTS

INTRODUCTION

Biography is great fun!

Biography is one of the most exciting forms of writing because it contains all the thrill of the chase. In many ways you are playing the detective. You have got the body – your subject – and frequently they *are* dead. It is your job to piece together the events that happened before this point. You need to examine all the evidence you can lay your hands on, interview any witnesses, visit the locations, read any written statements and finally give your verdict on the life.

You don't have to be an expert to be a biographer. Expert in what? Perhaps one of the best attributes for the would-be biographer is curiosity – some might say nosiness! People are interesting. Their actions are fascinating as the enormous popularity of the nightly soap operas on television testifies. Aspiring biographers need to be intrigued by people and the motives for their actions.

Do you need a degree in history to be a biographer? No. What you do require is lots of common sense, an enthusiasm for your subject and a dollop of good luck. Fortunately there is usually an allocation set aside for us!

Is it nosiness? Is it literature? Is it playing God?

In the end it is a mixture of all three. You are going to pry into your subject's most intimate secrets. You may well require details of their sex life, their private fears and deepest emotions. You will be the one who seeks out their diaries and the letters they might wish they had destroyed.

Yet, at its best, biography is a much-respected form of literature. Not only does it enhance our knowledge and understanding of some great people in our history, it is also a carefully crafted art form that uses language creatively. For me the best biographies portray the character so well, I feel that I know exactly how they would react if they were to walk through my door.

The biographer, however, does carry an enormous responsibility. You act like God on the Day of Judgement because you are examining a life. You weigh up the evidence and you sentence your subject to eternal praise or damnation through the medium of history. It is awesome! If I thought too hard about it I could get quite neurotic and would never dare to write anything. In the end the biographer has a duty to the reader and the subject to be truthful and fair. And that does not mean hiding the things you don't like. It means tackling them and trying to understand what was going through your subject's mind.

Writing the definitive biography

Well you can't! Although publishers like to advertise a book as the definitive biography of ..., it will not be. Someone else can always come along in the future and write another biography of that person. And it will be different. This instantly throws up the question, which book is telling the truth? Probably both are. The established facts concerning the subject's life have not changed, but may well be open to different interpretations. You have only to listen to both sides in an acrimonious divorce case to hear the truth being told, yet sounding different. So if you have tarnished the halo of some great person by your biography, don't get paranoid. They are likely to get a reworking in the future which may restore the sheen.

Biography is not history – it is closer to fiction!

I am not advocating that you make it up as you go along. Nor that you invent the details you could not unearth in order to make your narrative flow more smoothly. But biography is distinctly different from history. And it is worth spending a few moments considering how the two are different because you need to be clear in your own mind if you are going to produce good biographical writing. In many ways the biographer is the entertainer. When a reader picks up a book they are looking for a good story, written in such a way that they want to keep turning the pages to discover what happens next. The bald facts that you get in a history book, stating for example that a certain person went to Cairo in 1844, simply will not do for a biography. The reader wants to know what Cairo would have looked like, smelt like – even tasted like, if you can manage it! – and how the subject reacted. The biographer cannot take refuge in saying, 'How do I know? I wasn't there.'

This is where you need the techniques of fiction, but employed without telling any lies. Difficult? Yes. A challenge? Absolutely. But that's why biography is such fun. If you have to research mid-nineteenth century Egypt, and Cairo in particular, then use that information to dramatize your subject's arrival into this alien environment. Your reader wants to be there, seeing the scene through the subject's eyes. At this stage in your work, you will probably have a fair idea how your character reacted to new experiences, so put yourself in their position. Speculate/make an educated guess/invent it. What's the difference? A very narrow line! Remember though, the biographer who refuses to speculate fails the reader. If they had wanted a straight historical account they would have chosen one.

And another thought before you dive into that research headlong. Can I remind you of an incident well known to most of us?

Humpty Dumpty sat on a wall
Humpty Dumpty had a great fall
All the King's horses and all the King's men
Couldn't put Humpty together again.

That is the historian's account of the last moments in Mr Dumpty's life. It is a dispassionate statement of an event which must have been traumatic for the gentleman. The biographer starts here! An account like this poses many questions. The immediate one – did he jump or was he pushed? Or is there another possible explanation of Mr Dumpty's accident? The report we have is so matter-of-fact, it could hide a multitude of dirty deeds. What about observers of his accident? What would they say? As Humpty's biographer you need to read and listen to all the accounts of his demise in order to arrive at the truth.

You must establish what Humpty was doing on that wall anyway. I'm particularly curious about the involvement of the King's men.

Was Mr Dumpty connected with royalty? Check that out. And what part did the horses play in this? Research needed into the political situation at the time. From the evidence we are given, did the royal troops try sufficiently hard to reassemble Mr D? What methods did they use and what other methods of sticking eggs together were commonly in use at the time? Research needed here. And lastly, is it possible that they preferred Humpty Dumpty NOT to be put together again?

I have destroyed any charm this nursery rhyme might have had, but I hope it has given you an insight into the biographer's method.

Autobiography

Autobiography is an interesting form of biography since the writer is also the subject. Is it easier to write than biography? That is debatable. Obviously you have the research at your fingertips or perhaps locked in your brain. But how accurate are your memories? And does it matter anyway? Surely what the reader is interested in is the author's version of events, misguided or otherwise. Whilst autobiographical research and writing share many similarities with biography, in certain crucial areas they are different and so there is a special chapter devoted to this art form.

Writing up family history

This again has similarities with biography writing, but is a more specialized form that is reliant on a larger amount of historical data. For valuable advice on researching family history, you would do well to consult *Teach Yourself Tracing Your Family History* by Stella Colwell. For suggestions on presenting family history and writing it up in a literary form, there is a special chapter in Part Two of this book.

Read! Read! Read!

Whilst this book can offer you lots of advice and tips about biographical research and writing, you still need to read the works of acknowledged masters of this artform. Writers like Richard Ellman, Antonia Fraser, Michael Holroyd and Margaret Forster have all written much praised biographies for example. But look at your own sphere of interest as well. If you are writing about a military figure in the Falklands conflict then read a similar biography. If you are working on the unauthorized biography of a media figure then read how Kitty Kelly handled similar subjects. Not only can you see at first hand how the author dealt with issues, you can also judge how you, as a reader, reacted to what was written.

You don't have to read all the books cover to cover, scan read or dip into them in bookshops and libraries. Make sure you what you read is recent biographical writing. Few publishers want a revival of the Victorian style of hero-worship.

And finally ...

Human beings are endlessly fascinating, so researching and writing about them is marvellous fun. Enjoy yourself!

Part One –
RESEARCHING

1 | CHOOSING YOUR SUBJECT

Where do ideas come from?

Although this might appear to be a very sensible place to start a book about researching and writing a biography, it is also quite likely that many people reading this book will feel they do not need such a chapter. The reason you are interested in biography writing in the first place is probably because you have *already* got a good subject and want to know what to do next. Maybe a person has fascinated you with their extraordinary life or amazing achievements and you want to discover what makes them tick. Perhaps they have chosen you!

It certainly happened that way for me. I would never have considered writing biography because I was under the illusion that I needed some special qualifications. However, I bought a copy of *The Country Diary of an Edwardian Lady* six months after it was published and was enchanted. That was nothing unusual. Lots of other people were too. But I was most intrigued by the woman behind the book. She had painstakingly recorded her own nature observations in 1906 and yet had given away nothing about herself. It was curiosity on my part – nosiness if you prefer. I wanted to know more about the woman behind the diary. With absolutely no experience or contacts in the writing world, I started.

Even if you do already have a good subject this time, maybe in the future you will be looking for someone to study next. Here are a few tips about selecting a subject.

Anniversaries

Checking on anniversaries is a favourite ploy of professional biographers hunting for a marketable subject. If you can look ahead and spot the centenary of some great person or of an invention, for instance, it is likely there will be public interest at that time. The topic could well be featured in a magazine or television programme and that means instant publicity, a ready market for a book perhaps.

If you are searching for possible subjects, then a general reference book like *Pears Cyclopaedia* is a good place to begin. The biographical section lists briefly a large number of people plus dates, it also covers many disciplines and various nationalities. The names can then be investigated in greater detail. You could consult the entry in the *Encyclopaedia Britannica* for a great explorer or a biographical medical dictionary for a famous surgeon. *Who's Who* and *Who Was Who* or the many-volumed *Dictionary of National Biography* may well be the next step for British subjects. Note down any further references at the end of these entries so you can follow them up later.

For an American subject a number of resources will prove useful. Try, for example, the *Dictionary of American Biography* (available in 21 volumes), *Who's Who in American Women*, *Who's Who in American Politics* or *Who's Who in America*, to name but a few.

Time scale

If you are scanning anniversaries you need to look well ahead. A biography of a great composer that is offered for publication a year after the anniversary of his birth is about as attractive as a Christmas card that arrives on 30 December. I would suggest looking at least three years ahead, more preferably. That gives you two years for researching and writing, and a further year for publication. If you need to look for a publisher as well, you should add on at least another year.

I would not be comfortable working to a tighter time scale. There are so many things outside the writer's control. What if that vital letter you need to read, written by your subject's lover, is held in a collection on the other side of the world? You send your money off for the promised photocopy and three months later you are still waiting. When you chase them the reply is: the archivist is on maternity leave/the department is being reorganized/we have no record of your enquiry/the staff are all volunteers and working as fast as they can and so on. If, and when, you ever receive the photocopied letter, there is always the possibility that it might contain information that radically alters your perception of your subject. That could mean rewriting a large part of the text, which takes time.

The other factor outside your control is the publisher. First of all you have to find one who wants your book – never the easiest thing to do! Even the publisher who eventually accepts the manuscript may have been slow responding to your initial overtures (by slow I mean taking more than three months to read and reply to your draft material). Once accepted, there is still editorial and design work, as well as printing, to be done. And finally they will allocate a publication date that fits into *their* publishing schedule. So give yourself plenty of time.

Whilst anniversaries are a useful way of finding a subject, remember others are probably trawling through the biographical dictionaries with the same aim.

The local hero or heroine

Never despise the local subject. It is possible your village, town or county was the birthplace of somebody famous. Rags to riches yarns have a perennial appeal, like Cinderella or the poor barrow boy who becomes head of a multi-national company and achieves a millionaire lifestyle. People love reading about that sort of thing because deep down lurks the notion it could be them. There are also many advantages to the local subject. Don't underestimate the benefits of having at least some of the research on your doorstep. As a local you may know of folklore about your hero. There is usually somebody around who will say, 'My old dad said the Tennysons kept their horses down our stables.' Or, 'My granny used to clean for them when she was a young girl.' Then you are off! These are the sort of valuable personal contacts that the professional biographer living 200 miles away will never stumble upon. Talking to old Fred, whose great-grandad worked for your hero, could unearth the odd letter, picture or scandal that was previously unknown.

Your local hero or heroine does not necessarily have to be a 'great name'. They may be credited with having discovered a new star or invented some household object; yet little may be known about them. This could be your starting point. Maybe in the end you will decide to write a magazine article rather than a full-scale book. That does not matter, it is still worthwhile. Your work could spark off a renewed interest in the person.

Places

Places you visit may provide you with inspiration for a biography. My second book *Victorian Sisters* was the direct result of a visit to Wightwick Manor, a British National Trust property near Wolverhampton. On a visit there several years earlier I had noticed portraits of the Macdonald sisters. These four women had always been overshadowed by famous sons (Rudyard Kipling and Stanley Baldwin) or by famous husbands (Burne-Jones and Poynter). At the time I was intrigued by the relationships involved and several years later recalled these women when I was thinking about a potential subject for a book.

Ghost-writing

This is not some spooky art form as the name might suggest and neither does it involve writing about someone who is dead. Ironically ghost-writing is concerned with the living!

A famous person (or someone who is not famous but has a story to tell) may not feel capable of writing a book themselves. Instead they could ask you. In effect you are the person who holds the pen for them. In reality it involves far more than that: listening, selecting the material and arranging it, possibly checking facts and researching background material to set an event in its context. Admittedly most of the research is already done for you. The subject is there, pouring out their story into your listening ear. It is also likely they will have family pictures, certificates, press cuttings and other memorabilia.

Is this the easiest form of biography? I'm not so sure. You are not a free agent. You are working *for* the subject, at their request, and you should have drawn up some sort of agreement about your role, copyright (if it is to be published), costs and payment. The UK Society of Authors publishes an extremely helpful *Quick Guide to Ghost-Writing and Collaboration Agreements* which can be bought by non-members. It is well worth reading before you embark on such a project, so you are aware of what legal areas need clarifying.

As the ghost writer, it's your job to put down what your subject tells you, even if you do not agree that it is correct. Equally you have to leave out the parts they want to omit and give the whole work the slant they request – true or false!

At worst, it is a job and you have to provide the goods that your employer has paid for. At best, it can be a very enjoyable experience. I recently worked on the reminiscences of an octogenarian who had been a travelling lady's maid in the 1920s, accompanying her ladyship to exotic locations like China and Indonesia. Interviewing this lady to gather the material was a sheer delight and taught me a great deal in the process. The resulting work was never intended for publication, simply as a record for her family; nevertheless it was a pleasure to do.

Dead or alive?

After the ghost-writing, this seems an appropriate topic. Is it better to choose a subject who is alive or one who is dead? The subject who is alive has the advantages outlined previously and, added to that, their friends and family are there to talk to you. The more recent the subject, the better the chance that there are letters, pictures, video recordings and so on still available.

Do you need the subject's permission to write a biography? Surprisingly not, although I am sure there are many media personalities and royals who wish you did! Publication of the unofficial biography always has an air of the forbidden about it. But if you do choose to write about a subject who is still alive you must take enormous care. The *living* can pursue the biographer for libel!

Libel

Obviously the facts of a life are *facts* and usually beyond dispute; not so the interpretation or inference you put on them. This is the bit that is potentially libellous. Even if the subject agrees with your treatment of them in the book there are the friends and family to consider. They too can sue for libel if they believe you have made defamatory statements about them.

There is another difficult area to think about: that of passing judgement on the living, who have got to carry on with their lives after your book is published. Would you write the truthful, but harmful, details about a family? Expose the father's secret affair with the next-door neighbour 10 years earlier? Or the sister's childhood shop-lifting offences? You will always find ex-friends ready to provide you with the ammunition. But do you want to be responsible for firing the gun?

I suppose I am a coward for taking refuge in the dead. They cannot sue for libel, no matter what I write about them. And what is more, I like them well and truly dead! Fifty years is fine for the dust to settle and not just in the morbid sense either. After half a century you stand a fair chance of viewing the life in perspective. Hindsight always gives the best vision.

I was aware of this when I was writing about George Eliot fleeing from Britain to Germany with her lover George Henry Lewes in 1854. Had there been tabloids at the time, the headlines would have screamed *Woman editor seduces married man* or *Father of five abandons pregnant wife*, depending whom they judged to be the villain. Over a century later we view it differently. The wronged wife actually had three children by her husband and two by his best friend. George Eliot's affair with Lewes lasted 23 years until his death, and with his support she became one of Britain's greatest novelists.

Attitudes

Should you be in love with your subject?

This may seem a strange idea, but because biography is not history, it is worth weighing up your attitude towards your subject. Whether you like it or not, this will affect how you treat them. I think it is vital to examine your attitude towards them at various stages in your work. They are, or were, human beings and your attitude towards them will change, just as it would if you met them at different stages of their life.

You certainly do not have to be in love with your subject. In fact that would produce a very unconvincing biography. Remember the old adage *Love is blind*. There would be a temptation to turn your subject into a saint, a goody-goody who never set a foot wrong. Equally, writing a biography about someone you hate is just as dangerous. You might see their every action tainted with evil.

It is not love the biographer needs, but *admiration* for the person and their achievements: that, I think, is vital. The odds are that your research will reveal a human being with the same weaknesses and foibles that beset us all. At times you will be exasperated by your subject's actions, bewildered by their insensitivity, incredulous at their stupidity. At other times you will be amazed by their daring, full of praise for their achievement and love them for their humanity.

I will admit there is a problem if you reach a stage in your research where you really have lost all respect for your subject. What do you do if they turn out to be the sort of person you wouldn't want anything to do with? Well you may not have been in love with them, but I think it is time for divorce! Once respect has gone, it is hard to deal fairly with your subject. If you are tied into a contract with a publisher, it is definitely time to talk. It is possible that the publisher would actually like an iconoclastic biography – something to cut this great figure down to size. I don't think that I would like to do that, not because I am frightened of the reviews, rather I don't trust myself. If I dislike them that much, I am quite likely to ascribe all manner of evil intentions to even the most innocent of actions.

Out of the blue

As in all forms of creative writing, it is amazing where ideas come from. Even if these suggestions don't furnish you with a subject, a chance comment by a friend might set off a train of thought; a newspaper article or item on television could spark an interest. Choose your subject carefully; above all their life must make a good story.

TRY THIS
- ■ Find three possible subjects who will have anniversaries within the next five years.
- ■ What people, past or present, would make potential biography subjects in your country?

2 | STARTING YOUR RESEARCH

What has been published?

A good place to start is with what has already been published about your subject; not just the person themselves, but their friends, associates and indeed the whole field of study. These are *secondary sources* – other writers' opinions of the subject, based on their examination of the facts (see Chapter 10). These accounts are useful to the biographer because eventually they should lead you to the *primary sources*. Primary sources are first-hand accounts of your subject – the raw materials you need to work with (see Chapter 9). Simply chewing over someone else's opinions without reference to the original source does not produce a worthwhile study.

Go to a library

A good way to discover what has been published is to go to a library, preferably a large city library that has a separate reference section. Even though I don't live near one, I find it is worth making a day's expedition to kick things off. There you will be able to scan catalogues, microfiche or computerized records of virtually everything that has been published. It is also likely that you will be able to call up some of these texts to examine. The library is a better place to begin than a bookshop because bookshops are only able to tell you what is currently in print. Whilst you do need to know if someone has just published the biography you were going to write, when it comes to research, you want to know about books that are probably out of print.

Keep in mind also that you are interested in *everything* published about your subject, not only in the UK and the USA but also elsewhere in the world. Whilst a library may have English language publications, it may not hold those published elsewhere but can often order them for you.

If your subject is very specialized, you may have to think in terms of contacting a specialist library for help. There are all manner of small, but immensely useful specialist libraries around. (I have used, for example, ones specializing in dentistry, Unitarians and British India.) But start with the large public library first. The staff are usually extremely helpful and knowledgeable and may well be able to direct you to other sources.

Note it down

As you scan the lists of possible books, note down the *title*, *author*, *publisher* and *year* of anything that might conceivably be useful. If the library possesses a copy, note down any *catalogue numbers* or *search references*, even if you don't intend to look at the book on that visit. Keep this information filed. It can save so much time in the future.

Try to think around the subject. Note down information about any other possible biographies or books that may assist you to flesh out your character or period.

A large library will also hold reference dictionaries and these are worth consulting at an early stage. *The Dictionary of National Biography* is an obvious lead, *Who's Who* and *Who Was Who*, *Burke's Peerage*, *Crockford's Clerical Directory* (for Anglican clergy), as well as specialist dictionaries such as *The Dictionary of Victorian Watercolour Artists* may be helpful. Make detailed notes, or better still photocopy entries. It is amazing how some time later a seemingly unimportant snippet gains significance. It might simply be the name of the contributor, which meant nothing to you at the time, but later turns out to be your subject's brother-in-law.

Publications can also take the form of newspapers, magazines, specialist journals and leaflets. A large reference library may have copies or listings of these, but it is probable that you will have to search further. A medical library is more likely to have nineteenth-century copies of *The Lancet* than a county library. Eventually you may need to consult the holdings of the British Library at their Newspaper Library (Colindale Avenue, London, NW9 5HE), or the Library of Congress for back copies of newspapers and periodicals you cannot track down. But it is also worth remembering that the branch library near your subject's home may well have humble publications like parish magazines (which could easily go back a century) or other small scale publications with useful information.

What do you read?

This is always difficult. If you discover lots of biographies about your subject, do not attempt to read them all. What you are interested in is the back of the book: you want to know the author's sources. But it is advisable to read the most up-to-date study of your subject for two reasons. At some stage you have got to produce an outline of the person's life, and secondly, you need to know what sort of approach the biographer took. Scan earlier studies for the date, author and their pedigree. Was he or she a friend of the subject rather than a professional biographer? If so, that book may well yield very different information and I would certainly want to read a biography written by a contemporary. Scan other books quickly. Try to get an idea of what slant the writer took and what audience he or she envisaged. I remember being very disappointed when I collected the biography of Marie Curie I had ordered from a bookshop having read the title in a catalogue, only to discover it was written for junior school children.

In the case of most sources you consult, I would advise photocopying the bibliography, sources and acknowledgements for future reference.

Don't dismiss locally produced studies. They can often yield interesting insights into your character and give you hints about things to follow up later. Never underestimate local knowledge. In the past I have found that the university professor who wrote a biography sitting in his study, sending students to chase up references, overlooked the humble sources which yielded new information and new pictures.

Photocopy the contemporary newspaper accounts if you can. Failing that, make detailed notes, even the bits you can't make sense of – they may fall into place later and you don't want to waste time returning to that source again.

Bibliographies

Study with great care! Photocopy whenever possible. This is what will lead you to the primary sources – the letters, the diaries and the relatives. This part of the book, usually just before the index, is far more valuable to you than any interpretation the author gave of the subject. You want to be able to read the facts yourself and form your own conclusions. It is not just earlier biographies you are looking for in the bibliography, but information about your subject's friends, interests etc. The books that the biographer consulted for their background research may give you clues.

Besides books there may be a separate listing for journals, with volume numbers and page references. These could be recent writings that contain articles about your field of study or contemporary ones that featured your subject. For example, *The Studio* magazine of 1902 may have reported an exhibition of the subject's paintings with, perhaps, an illustration. It is not as difficult to consult early journals as you might think. Most libraries (even the local branch ones) can order photocopies of relevant sections of the most obscure publications for a nominal payment. The advantage is that you get to keep the photocopy and can mark sections up with a highlighter pen if you like.

A bibliography may well list primary sources separately from published works. This is where you will get to see what letters, diaries and family papers exist (as well as other unpublished information like military records) and where they are held. Check this carefully at the back of every biography or study you come across, in case there is material in one that is not in another.

Once you have got the names of the archives, write to them requesting a more detailed list of their holdings. At the same time ask about visiting to read material and the availability of photocopies or loan of microfilm so that you do not have to waste time with a further letter should the material prove useful to you.

Acknowledgements

These are likely to be at the front of a book. Once again study with care and photocopy if at all possible. This is where the author thanks everyone who has helped them. Admittedly this can be their wife, granny, typist and the family dog, but it should also contain the names of public institutions that helped. Here you may well learn of the existence of a tiny library, a support group or some organization that has a specialist interest in eighteenth-century Italian wines, for example. You are also looking for evidence of present day descendants of your subject. Those with the same surname are easy to spot but married names hide people. This is where the photocopy comes in useful. At a later stage in your research you may discover that the sister married a Fullbrook and, lo and behold, that surname turns up in someone else's acknowledgements.

Making contact

Once you have got the names of organizations, libraries, professional societies, fan clubs, relatives and so on, you start the letters. Who do you write to? Absolutely anyone who might know something – just in case! As a biographer, it is your greatest fear that you may have left a stone unturned.

Keep your initial letter clear and simple. You are trying to discover if they can be of any help to you first. If the reply is promising, you can follow it up with more specific enquiries.

TRY THIS
- Look at the acknowledgements in a biography and see if you can identify any possible relatives or descendants.
- What specialist libraries or institutions did the author consult?

3 | FILING YOUR RESEARCH

Devising a system

As answers begin to flow in from the letters you sent out and as you start to amass notes, it is vital to file everything methodically. In the early days it might seem pretentious to start a file with loads of headings, when you have only got one sheet to go in some sections and nothing in most of them. But after six months of research there will be all sorts of information, on all shapes and sizes of paper: photocopies, small handwritten letters, photographs, file paper, scraps from notepads, faxes, picture postcards and scribbled notes on the backs of old envelopes. For your own sanity, and ease of research, you have to devise a method of storing this information in a form you can easily retrieve.

There are all sorts of different systems for filing information, but the essence is to devise one that suits you. Your system basically needs to fulfil two functions:

1 You need to store paper so that it does not get lost.
2 You need to be able to lay your hands easily on any piece of paper at a later date.

Beginning to file research

As you have no idea what sort of material will be coming in, it is best to begin with one simple ring binder file. Hole-punch most of your paperwork, and use thin plastic wallets to include pictures or material you don't want to damage with holes. As the material grows, insert dividers into the file to separate different topics. It may be that you decide to file research notes separately from letters and written reports of interviews, but later you may find it more convenient to arrange the material under topics that relate to your subject's life. The headings might well be things like: *ancestors*; *childhood*; *schooling*; *marriage* or it might be that divisions like *Sandhurst* and *Sienna* are more relevant.

My filing system is evolutionary! By that I don't mean it began in the Stone Age, although people who use computer databases would probably think so. What I mean is that the system develops as I work. From a single ring binder file, I move to dividers. Then as each division grows, it may move to its own file and later occupy a large lever-arch file or spawn a second volume. Equally, some divisions may disappear or be subsumed into another section as they prove less significant than expected.

Filing different types of material

Letters

In the early days of research a useful section might be *letters*. Copies of your letters could be grouped together and the replies filed alongside as they come in. This makes it easy for you to keep tabs on your progress and decide when to chase things up. However, later on you might find it more helpful to distribute the letters into the sections that deal with that part of the subject's life. So the letter to the Local History Group enquiring about the cottage where the subject was born moves to the *childhood* section.

It is important to keep a copy of the letters you send out in case, at a later date, you want to know whether you did ask a certain question, or perhaps whether you phrased your request clearly enough to elicit the answer you wanted.

Notes

The notes made from library books can sometimes be hard to categorize because they may cover more than one topic. The best thing to do then is to choose the most appropriate place to file the notes, but at the same time put a sheet detailing the source, basic content and place where you have filed this information into other relevant sections just to remind yourself that this research exists.

Quotations

With research notes it is absolutely vital to write down the title, author, publisher and date of the book you used. If you copy any quotations down, thinking they may come in useful in the future, take enormous care to copy them precisely – right down to the exact punctuation of the original. And, just as vital, note down the page number where the quotation appeared in the book. If the reference quoted in the book was from an original source, note down all the details given about that source too, *as well as* the page number of the book you found it in. In the early days of research these things seem tedious, especially as you can probably remember which book it was in, even what colour the cover was! Two years later when the manuscript is nearing completion, you may not be so sure and it is an absolute pain trying to get hold of the book again, just to check whether it was a colon or semi-colon in the quotation. And yes, it does matter that you are this precise in your work.

Odd comments penned at the top of your notes, stating where you saw the book, might come in handy. Sometimes it is hard to remember whether the 1896 edition you used was in a city Reference Library, or was it shown to you by the great niece you interviewed? It may be vital to know if you have some checking to do at editorial stage, when time is of the essence.

Cross-referencing

Some people like their filing system to fulfil more than just storage and retrieval functions, they also want to cross-reference information. If they look up the word *Lichfield*, for instance, they will find a list of pictures of the city that they have assembled; notes about buildings in the city; information about Erasmus Darwin's connection and the location of a recipe for a Lichfield cake. Cross-referencing information is quite a complex procedure and needs to be carried out each time something new is added to your file. You can use small index cards, a tabulated notebook or, if you are hi-tech, a computer database. It is very much a matter of personal inclination. I prefer a lo-tech system of filing and rely on my head for cross-referencing, but I know of other biographers who find a card index essential.

Pictures

Don't forget that pictures also require careful filing. You may want to refer to an etching when you are writing, in order to create a written image of the house your subject lived in. Or you may want to use a copy of that picture in your finished book, so information about that illustration is extremely important. Note the source of every picture and any information you can glean about its ownership, permissions for reproduction, copyright, date when it was taken or painted, information about the subject matter etc. All these things should be recorded on a sheet, filed alongside the illustration.

To sum up, file everything associated with your research, even the scrappy notes (complete with doodles) that you made on the phone when you arranged an interview. It is strange how, at a later date, some odd comment your interviewee made takes on a significance you had never anticipated. Similarly it is useful to note the date at the top of the report of any interview or visit you carried out. I admit it is likely that much of this information will never be used, but the difficulty is that you don't know which bits will be important until the end of the project.

File everything – you never know what will come in handy!

TRY THIS
■ Choose a subject and decide on the most helpful headings for filing your research.

4 | HISTORICAL BACKGROUND

Setting your subject in context

A carefully researched historical background is essential for a successful biography. If you think back to the biographies you enjoyed the most, it is probable that the subject came alive *and* you gained a real flavour of the period. Your research is important if the subject lived long ago, say in Tudor times, but well-chosen details about the pace of life in the Swinging Sixties or the anxieties of rural life during the First World War may help the reader to engage with the subject and their everyday dilemmas.

Working on the historical background also enables you, the author, to understand the subject's reaction to situations. Don't worry if you are ignorant of Parisian life in the 1890s or the situation which led to the Great Depression of the 1930s. You can learn. Most biographers have to read up some historical background for their project, even those who specialize in writing about a particular period. They may be familiar with the political scene, but they still have to study the local history that relates to their subject.

Creating a timeline

This is a very simple device which you should set up for the main character in every biography you work on. It is basically a list of the personal events in the subject's life, written in chronological order and set alongside local and national events.

You need a couple of sheets of A4 lined file paper. In the margin you write every year of your subject's life. It is often helpful to begin the timeline about five years before their birth, just in case there were any significant events that impinged on their childhood: the family became bankrupt; a sibling died or a major war broke out shortly before their birth. It is helpful to leave a line or two between each year so that, if there is a particularly busy year, you have got space to fit everything in. Failing that, sellotape another sheet onto the right-hand side.

The timeline usually ends with the subject's death, but it can be useful to run it on a bit further – you may want to track the progress of children or the posthumous success of your subject's work.

Adding the age of the subject against each year is marvellous for quick reference. You can see at a glance that he was actually 50 when he first met the love of his life, or that her first poem was published when she was 16, in the same year that her mother died.

A timeline helps you to keep events in perspective. When you are focusing on someone's life, it is easy to forget the wider picture and fail to notice that, at the time of the affair with that French actress in London, the Bastille was being stormed in Paris.

The national background

It is vital that you know what was going on nationally and have an awareness of major international events at the time your subject was alive. You could argue that your subject, living deep in the countryside in the sixteenth century, was totally unaware of these events, but the reader isn't. Information like this helps the reader to set the topic into the wider context of history. It is intriguing for the reader to realize that, as the subject of the biography trod the boards at the Haymarket, the British Parliament was voting through the Great Reform Bill.

How do you glean this knowledge? Don't panic! When it is a period you know very little about, you get a school textbook as a starter – junior school level if need be! Usually though, a secondary level history textbook is ideal. It is reasonably easy to read and deals with the period in sufficient depth.

For most eventualities the school textbook will suffice, but you may find areas that require more detailed research. The father of one of my characters was farming at the time of the Corn Laws, so that called for further investigation to understand where the family stood on this contentious issue. For more detailed research into English history you could move to the relevant volume of the

Oxford History of England, which is readily available in libraries. The *Dictionary of American History* and *The Annals of America* are two series that could be particularly useful when researching American history.

It is sensible to begin researching around the time of your subject's birth, or as mentioned a few years earlier. Not only is starting at the beginning logical, but it will enable you to set the birth in context. After a bit of study, you might discover an excellent opening to your biography: 'As Capitol Hill prepared to welcome a new president, in a ranch in Wyoming a baby boy was born who would change the face of American politics.'

Local background

In many ways the local historical background is even more important in a biography than the national scene. After all, it is usually neighbourhood squabbles and scandals which are the meat of daily conversation over the garden gate or at the breakfast table.

If you have no knowledge of the locality seek help from the reference department of the county library, or their local studies department. They will be able to tell you what has been written about the area, both published and unpublished. They may even put you in touch with a local history group or an amateur historian. Never underestimate local knowledge. In my experience the amateur historian who works for love, not money, has often devoted years to this study and left few stones unturned. They are often very willing to share information and work with you, whereas the professional can be suspicious of someone else's interest and may not volunteer information willingly. The professional can have various other projects on the go and may actually know less than the local amateur.

You need to be clear in your mind what sort of information you require, so you don't vanish underneath a welter of fascinating but irrelevant facts. You may want to know something about employment in the area to understand where the family stood in the local hierarchy (a polite way of saying what class they were). Information about housing in the area can give you a lot of clues. Street directories can be helpful. Many contain a thumb-nail sketch of the hamlet, village or town they go on to list.

Looking at contemporary maps is useful and the larger the scale, the better. Try to photocopy relevant sections if you can, so that you have something beside you as you work. Later this will enable you to describe how your subject walked past the old stone church and the knacker's yard every day on his way to school. Such information may help you to work out why many of his early poems contained the agonized cries of animals.

Remember that the site of your local history research will have to change if your subject leaves their childhood haunts for the big city. You may suddenly require details about life in London in the mid-nineteenth century. And off you go again!

Specific historical research

The particular field in which your subject achieved eminence will need specific research. For a Victorian actress, you will need details of nineteenth-century theatre. As mentioned before, acknowledgements and bibliographies in books may guide you to other books and societies. The reference departments of large city libraries can check to see whether there is a specialist theatre library, say, or an Ellen Terry Society, or whatever specialism you require.

As you work, the unexpected often turns up. In the diary of one of my subjects there was a reference to a girl having her tooth extracted 'under the influence of electricity'. That sounded interesting. I mentioned it to my dentist next time I was in for a check-up and asked if he had any ideas. He didn't, but he gave me the address of the dental archive. A couple of letters later, I had the necessary information about this barbaric method of administering electric shocks at the same time as pulling teeth out. It was wonderful material, which enabled me to dramatize the incident to the full in my book, giving the reader a real feel of the period!

All this historical research might sound formidable, but it's not really. Don't attempt to do it all at the outset. You can't for one thing, because you don't know what you need to know! Concentrate on the birth and early years first. Gradually assemble details about the national and local scene that you could work into the text when you start writing. As your subject moves on either geographically or simply chronologically, research the next section. Be heartened, it's far easier than it might sound. It is also amazingly interesting. I never knew about electrical dentistry before!

TRY THIS

- Construct a timeline for your subject with national events included.
- Which events on your timeline will need particular research?

---

5 | INTERVIEWS

Meeting people

Now comes the exciting part: meeting the friends and family of your subject or their descendants. It's fun because there is now a personal element to your work, whereas previously you were ploughing through documents. Meeting people associated with your subject, however distantly, brings the character to life. It also gives you the opportunity to ask questions – mind you, there's no guarantee you will get any answers! With documentary research you can only work with what is in front of you, but now you have the chance to be a little more creative. You can choose what to ask and which lines to pursue.

Who do you want to talk to?

Ideally, you want to talk to the closest relatives and friends of your subject or, failing that, their descendants. You may have spotted likely names in the acknowledgements of some books, but there will not be any addresses or any hint of where they live. Of course, if the book you were working from was published in 1926, there is every likelihood that the descendant you are interested in is now dead. Make sure that you are trying to track down someone who is likely to be still living!

How do you find them?

With a more recent publication, you could try writing to the author (via the publisher), to ask if they would forward a letter or supply you with the address. You could also try some of the organizations mentioned in the acknowledgements to see if they have had contact with the family. Send a self-addressed envelope whenever you are asking for help; people feel more inclined to respond.

If you know the area where a person lives, try the telephone directory or the electoral register. The register which covers that parliamentary ward can be consulted at a reference library. Or you might ask the local library if they know of the person you are seeking. They might, particularly if a famous relative is involved. Basically, keep asking any likely people you encounter – eventually somebody will know. Once you get a break-through, you are off. One lead may well turn into another and, if you are very lucky, two others.

Who's Who, a source which has already been mentioned, lists people's addresses, as well as the clubs they belong to. It might be worth looking there – past and present editions. You may be able to think of other listings that the descendants could be in. For instance they might appear in an exhibition list or some regimental record. Be prepared for the possibility that the person will have died just before you manage to locate them – such things do happen!

Another possible source of information might be a fan club, a literary society or support group. If your subject painted, published or designed buildings, for example, they may have been a member of a professional body. Ask these organizations if they know of any surviving relatives. Equally, a library or archive that holds papers relating to your subject may have contact with the present day family. I always look to see who deposited the papers in the first place, just in case it is a name that I was not aware of. Might the family possess other material not considered important enough for the archive? This is often the case. Medals and paintings go to the national collection but personal memorabilia are frequently retained. A pencilled account of the subject's childhood, their favourite toy and a dog-eared school exercise book all remain at home. A treasure trove to the biographer!

Still drawing a blank?

You could try the area where the subject last resided, even if it was a century ago. What happened to the house after your subject left? Was it sold? Who stood to gain? Do today's occupants have any knowledge or contacts? Check your subject's will to see who the beneficiaries were. That may also give you ideas of which descendants you need to pursue (see page 38).

Don't give up hope, just remain alert and check everything – the contributor of the *Dictionary of National Biography* entry, *Who's Who* names. I became aware of a descendant of the artist I was studying from reading the reverse of a birthday card: 'Reproduced by kind permission of ...' And there was someone with the same surname as the artist I was studying. Assisted by the card's publishers, I tracked down the grandson, who owned the remains of the family archive.

The meeting

Write and seek an interview with anyone you would like to meet. You can phone, but it is preferable not to put people on the spot. I think there is every likelihood they will say 'no' if you catch them on the hop. Then you have blown it. It is much harder to persuade them to change their mind after that. A carefully worded letter allows the person to consider your request at their leisure, and a self-addressed envelope persuades them to say 'yes'. Well that's my theory!

Explain how much you would appreciate their help and that you understand their time is valuable. Yes, I know that sounds creepy, but remember no one is obliged to see you. I keep it firmly in my head that the person is doing *me* a great favour. There is nothing in it for them. Also, if they are connected with someone famous, the chances are that I am not the first person to have pestered them. Amazingly, with very few exceptions, I have found the people I have approached to be incredibly kind, interested and hospitable. Several have continued as friends long after the book was finished.

Plan your questions

Assume that you will get only one chance to put your questions to the interviewee. Make the most of it. Do your homework carefully. The person you go to interview will assume that you are already very knowledgeable about their relative. So read all the information you have about the subject and their connection with the interviewee. It doesn't matter if you can't hold all the details in your head. Take your notepad to refer to – it looks professional so don't worry about it.

What you are seeking to find out are the personal details that will make your subject come alive; that they loved cats, had a great sense of humour, couldn't sit still for two minutes or hated foreigners. You want to hear the anecdotes that have been handed down through the family. This is the sort of information you will not come across anywhere else and it is usually all true.

Pictures

Whilst you are there, ask the interviewee if they have any pictures related to the topic – not just photographs of people. Things like the family home or the village at the turn of the century can be just as valuable to you. As well as pictures, ask about letters and memorabilia. Note details down carefully and consider whether it is worth taking a quick photograph with a pocket camera. Ask permission before you photograph anything. I remember being shown some silver sugar tongs that had once belonged to my subject. Not particularly exciting, I thought, but I noticed the hallmark was Edinburgh 1911. Later that made sense. My subject had spent a year studying with a Scottish artist and became friendly with the family. The sugar tongs were a wedding present from that same family some 20 years later.

How to start

What I usually do is chat informally to begin with. Many of the people I have interviewed have been elderly, often living alone, who are more than happy to talk. First though, they need to know a little about me if they are going to trust me with family information. So the interview usually begins with me. Am I married? Have I got any children? If I can see that they are very keen gardeners, I mention the problems I've been having with my wisteria this year, and so on. You'll probably be itching to get started on the business, but be patient. Building up trust is vital in the long run. To you the visit is business, to the interviewee it may be a social event.

When we move on to business, I get my reporter's style notepad out of my bag. I'll have a list of questions to kick things off. The difficult part is to chat and take notes as you go. My notes are scribbled in my own abbreviated form. After I've left the interview,

I often park just up the road and write it up or work on the train going home, whilst the conversation is still fresh in my mind. I find that even though I have not written everything they said, my scribbled notes are a good enough prompt for me to remember all the main points that were made. If I leave it a day or two before I write it up, I don't remember so accurately.

Tape recording or note-taking?

I do sometimes record interviews with a small cassette recorder and it is useful to be able to go through the contents again quietly at home. But I often find that my interviewees are inhibited by a recorder placed on the coffee table. The old lady who has agreed to see me, even invited me to lunch, is quite happy to chat informally about her great aunt Agatha, but clams up the instant she sees a tape recorder. This is not because she was going to tell me anything secret, but because the tape recorder seems official and she is frightened of saying something silly.

Even a tape-recorded interview needs to be listened to, sifted, then written up. It is worth putting the main points of the interview down on paper and filing them (see page 15). Your notes will jog your memory about the contents of the tape. If the interview proved really valuable, it is advisable to file a full transcript.

Don't forget to label the tape with:

- the date of interview
- the name of the interviewee
- the subject of the interview.

A good tip is to break the safety lug at the top of the tape as this prevents anyone accidentally taping over it.

And one final point of warning. Even though the interviewee spoke freely to you, should you choose to quote verbatim from your tape, you need their permission. The copyright of the words belongs to the speaker.

Filing notes

All interviews, whether taped or written as notes, should be filed in the appropriate spot. Head the interview with the name of the person involved and the date you interviewed them. Take care to write everything up. When I do this, I often think it is a waste of time, I can remember it anyway. Yet when I look back a year later and 20 interviews down the line, I am often surprised by information I wrote down and yet have no recollection of. Sometimes the throw-away comment I scribbled down takes on a new significance in the light of later research.

At the same time as writing up your interview, do write and thank the interviewee for their help and hospitality. Not only is it good manners, but you may want their help again and you need them to be favourably inclined towards you. It is also possible that your visit jogged the interviewee's memory and, after you left, they remembered something else. You want them to tell you that information as well.

Do you believe everything they tell you?

Unless they are being particularly devious, the interviewee is probably telling you what they *honestly believe*. That doesn't, of course, mean that it is *true*. As we all know, families have their own version of events which puts them in a good light. These stories are then handed down the generations. You may get conflicting information, but it is useful to know, for example, that the brother's family thought the marriage was unhappy, whereas the husband's family believed it to be blissful. Faced with contrary opinions, all you can do is note them down and look for further evidence. It is possible that both parties are telling the truth, but from different viewpoints.

If your research proves that one version is false, it can be useful to work out why the story was perpetuated. What someone at the time *thought* was the case, can often be just as revealing as what *actually* happened.

TRY THIS
- Work out which two people connected with your subject would be the most useful to interview.
- What questions would you use to open the interview?

---

6 DOCUMENTARY RESEARCH

Checking the facts

This is obviously a major area of research which is used to underpin the other evidence you gather. If an interviewee tells you when his father married or that he was killed in a war, you will need to check it against *official records*. This is not because interviewees often lie but because memories can be faulty. The 'chinese whispers' effect can distort a story as it is handed on, so documentary corroboration is important for accuracy and your credibility. This chapter will only cover a few of the commonly used documents. There are hundreds, most of which I have not had need of. Different periods of history and different areas of study require different types of document, but that's not a problem. As you work, you will come across areas that you need to verify or cross-check. One or two phone calls or a conversation with an archivist will usually point you in the right direction for the documents you need.

So sharpen your pencils, pack your sandwiches, fill your thermos flask and off you go. None of those things are quite as jokey as they might sound. Many record offices that permit access to original documents only allow researchers to use pencil. Some are in out-of-the-way places, close for lunch and turf you out, desperate for a cup of coffee. So it pays to be prepared!

Birth, marriage and death certificates

These are always the first documents that spring to mind in biography writing and it is true that they are important, not just for the subject of the book, but for many of the people closely associated with them. It never ceases to surprise me how much more you can glean from these documents beyond the mere date an event took place.

Compulsory registration of births, deaths and marriages came into force in 1837 in England and Wales, so that may restrict you depending on your subject. Fine of course for British Victorian subjects and subsequent ones, but no use for that biography of Admiral Lord Nelson or Queen Elizabeth I. You can consult the registration district where the event took place to obtain a copy of the certificate you require, but it may prove easier to consult The Family Records Centre, 1 Myddleton Street, Islington, London, EC1R 1UW. This can be done by post or by visiting the centre in person to consult the indexes and hunt through for the names that you require.

In the United States, the compulsory registration of births, marriages and deaths varies from state to state. Most of the older states required this by the first part of the twentieth century, but some were mid-century. County Court Houses in the states tended to keep early records of these occasions.

However, many genealogy libraries have been developed in the United States to make research of these documents easier. These can be found in most large cities, one of the largest being The Genealogy Library of the Church of Jesus Christ of Latter Day Saints, 50E North Temple, Salt Lake City, Utah 15140, USA.

Birth certificates

Even if you know the date of birth of your subject, it is still worth looking at the certificate because it contains other information. The place of birth is given, the name and sex of the child and information about the parents. The mother's maiden name is given (if applicable) and the father is usually named, along with his occupation. The addresses of the parents are also recorded. This information can be useful as it provides leads for your research into the parents.

Marriage certificates

Marriage certificates give the full names and ages of the couple, although sometimes a person may be described as *of full age*, which is irritating when you needed an exact age. All this means is that the person was over 21 if the certificate was issued prior to 1970 when the legal age was lowered to 18. The marriage certificate tells you that your subject was married before if they are described as widower, rather than bachelor. The couple's addresses at the time of their marriage are recorded which may open your research out further, as will the names and occupations of their fathers. From the marriage certificate you will also learn the names of the witnesses, the person who conducted the marriage and where it took place. The last piece of information might be helpful if you are trying to discover any religious affiliations, or lack of them.

Death certificates

In addition to the name and date of death of the deceased, the certificate will provide you with their occupation and last address as well as the cause and place of death. It can be worth looking to see who registered the death and what their relationship to the deceased was. This person is likely to be someone who was in close contact with the deceased and they might lead you to a hitherto unknown friend or relative.

Censuses

These are enormously valuable records but censuses started in Britain at much the same time as the registration of births, marriages and deaths, which can be frustrating if your subject flourished earlier. However, if you are working within their period, the census and the birth, marriage and death certificates can support or inform each other. Once you have located a person on the census returns, you will have a better idea of when and where to look for their certificates, although it has never ceased to amaze me how mobile people were in the past.

The census can be inspected freely after 100 years. It is usually held on microfiche at local record offices and county libraries but The Family Records Centre holds all the census returns for England and Wales.

The first census in Britain was actually 1801 but this was predominantly a numerical record. The first one that is useful to biographers is the 1841 one which was taken in June, thereafter they were in early April every 10 years. They vary a bit in the sort of information they recorded. Beware of ages on the 1841 census. Those under 15 had their exact age noted whilst those over 15 had their ages rounded down to the nearest five years (so someone of 34 would appear as 30). The 1841, 1851 and 1861 censuses showed the *last* job that a person did, but they may have retired or been out of work at the time of the census. I found the 1851–1881 censuses especially helpful in some of my research because they recorded how many people the householder employed or, in the case of a farmer, how many acres he farmed. This can give an indication of the status of a person. Bear in mind that it wasn't always the well-off who kept servants. Most of my subjects had servants, including a Methodist minister's family who were by no means well-off. A better guide to a family's affluence is the *number* of servants they employed, their *age* (young ones seemed to come cheap) and the *duties* specified.

There are always a few people who don't appear on the census for one reason or another, but who did exist. Usually the census gives details of everyone staying overnight at the residence. This can be helpful in finding out about 'invisible' people like servants, many of whom came and went on a regular basis.

The census return lists the householder, usually a senior male, and names his relations in the house, usually his wife and children. Any visitors on the night of the census will also be listed. For instance, the householder's niece may be listed. Initially you can't judge whether she just stayed for the night or whether she lived there because her mother died. Further research may put you right.

For every person listed their first name, age, place of birth, marital status and occupation is given. All are useful and the place of birth can help widen your research.

Don't be in too much of a hurry to leave the census returns after you have located the family you want. There are other useful bits of information there for the biographer. Look at the neighbours. This can give you an idea of what the locality was like. Read the occupations of those next door and up the road. Similarly, at the start of each section of the census there is a short description of the area, geographical rather than sociological, but very useful all the same. Augment the description with a photograph and you are beginning to discover what the place must have been like when your subject lived there. This is ideal material for your book.

It is worth trying to consult *every* census available for your subject's life. When you read them in order you may identify a rise or fall in social status or some other change.

The electoral register

Unlike many of the other documents mentioned, the electoral register is especially helpful for those working on modern biography. This document lists all the people resident at the property who are eligible to vote in Parliamentary elections, that is those aged over 18 since 1970 and over 21 since 1928. Prior to that women had the vote over the age of 30 after 1918 and men over 21 after 1884.

Again unlike most of the previous documents mentioned, up-to-date versions can be consulted. The current electoral register is held at the local Post Office and Reference Library of the relevant parliamentary ward. Previous registers are held at The Family Records Centre.

Parish registers

People often think these are not worth consulting if you have seen the birth, marriage or death certificate, but slightly different information may be given. The parish registers record any Christian rites that took place, which may be restricting if your subject had another, or no, religious affiliation. These records do have the advantage that they go back much further than the civil registration of birth, marriage and death. Theoretically, parish records in Britain can go back as far as 1538, though few survive from that time.

If you are interested in consulting these records you would be well advised to start with the county record office. Tell them which parish you are interested in – they can tell you what is available and where it is held. Nowadays most parish records have been deposited in the county office, but it is still possible to come across a church where they are kept in the vestry. I have a vivid memory from quite early in my biographical career. A churchwarden insisted on locking me in the vestry 'because you never know who is about'. I admit he left me with a key to let myself out, but he switched all the lights off in the church. I was left on my own in the church on a dismal, overcast November afternoon in the freezing cold. Then at the end of my search, I had to work my way across the dark church, with no idea where the light switches were, to let myself out. Scary!

Baptisms

Baptisms were sometimes recorded in a specific baptismal register and sometimes in a general one covering baptisms, marriages and funerals for that year. It's worth remembering that babies were not always baptized immediately after birth, though if their life was in danger they usually were. When hunting for a baptism, it is worth looking several years forward. Families sometimes 'did a batch together' if there were several children due for baptism. You may find the baptism register records the father of an illegitimate child, whereas the birth certificate doesn't. Perhaps the vicar was privy to a little local knowledge and decided to include it.

Illegitimate births

Although your research might have led you to an illegitimate birth with no obvious indication of who the father might be, don't despair. There may be a possible way of locating him. In former times the parish was extremely concerned about who would pay for the upkeep of illegitimate children and tried very hard to prove parentage, so the parish would not have to support the child. Some areas have 'bastardy returns' where the mother was interviewed about the father of her child and wherever possible a father was named on the documents.

Marriage

With the marriage register, remember that you should start looking for the wedding in the bride's parish. The entry is likely to carry much the same information as the official marriage certificate, largely because the minister was also the registrar. However, in the case of pre-1837 marriages there is no other record.

Burial

This is a burial rather than a death register and, as such, is unlikely to yield as much information as a death certificate. The cause of death is unlikely to appear but names, addresses, marital status and occupation should be there.

Information in the burial register may lead you to the actual gravestone and an inscription could add to your knowledge. Sadly, many graveyards have been cleared of their tombstones. This can be frustrating when you turn up keen to hunt for one, only to discover a neatly mown bowling green and not a grave in sight. However, sometimes county record offices have a plan of the graveyard and transcriptions of the tombstones before they were moved.

The parish chest, in practice or in theory (if papers have been moved for safe-keeping to the record office), may contain all manner of other miscellaneous documents. It is worth asking what else is recorded for the parish. One churchwarden's accounts gave me an interesting insight into life in the village in the 1840s: I learned my subject's father spent his time ridding the parish of hedgehogs, but I never found out why.

Nonconformist records

Much of the source material mentioned above is strongly linked to the Anglican church. Your subject may have had Nonconformist connections. This can be a blessing in disguise because the Nonconformists often kept better records than the established church. Much useful detail can be gleaned from the minute books of the Religious Society of Friends, known as Quakers. In the UK these can be consulted by application to the Library at Friends' House, Euston Road, London, NW1 2BJ; in the USA, try the Religious Society of Friends at Pendle Hill, 338 Plush Mill Road, Wallingford, PA 19086. Similarly Dr Williams's Library, 14 Gordon Square, London, WC1H 0AG houses the records for many other Nonconformist groups. And The Family Records Centre, which has already been mentioned, holds many Nonconformist registers from 1567–1837. You can find them on the Internet at http://www.pro.gov.uk

The International Genealogical Index

This index is the Mormon register and is often known by the initials IGI. The Mormons collected the data from a large number of parish registers and recorded them. The IGI is available on microfiche at The Family Records Centre but is frequently accessible to members of local family history societies, who might be willing to check some facts for you. It can also be accessed on the Internet: www.familysearch.org

Other sources

British citizens abroad

The Family Records Centre also holds some indexes of the birth, marriage and death of British citizens abroad from the late eighteenth century, including deaths in the two World Wars.

Divorce

Divorce may be relevant to your research. Indexes of divorces in the UK between 1858 and 1958 can be consulted at the Public Record Office, Ruskin Avenue, Kew, Richmond, Surrey, TW9 4DU. Legal divorce before 1858 was uncommon and only the province of the very wealthy since it involved an Act of Parliament.

To access divorce details in the USA, you should consult the public records of the local county court, or a volume such as the *Researchers' Guide to American Genealogy*.

Coroner's inquests

If your research leads you to an inquest, it may prove difficult to get access to official records because they remain closed for 75 years. Your best bet is to look in local newspapers, even national ones, to see if the event was deemed newsworthy. Details of what was said at an inquest are often reported.

Adoption

Your research might involve adoption. Indexes of legal adoption in England and Wales from the beginning of 1927 can be consulted at

The Family Records Centre. Anything earlier may need more specialized guidance.

Wills

In the UK The Family Records Centre holds some copies of wills from 1383–1858 but warns that only a minority of people left a will and 'only a minority of that minority left wills that are now held by the Public Record Office'.

Wills after 1858 are held at Somerset House, Strand, London, WC2R 1LP but a set of microfiche indexes for 1858–1943 can be consulted at The Family Records Centre.

Probate records are held at the Public Record Office and can be consulted once the appropriate reader's ticket has been obtained.

In the USA, wills are recorded in the local county court house.

War deaths

With the advent of the Internet, tracing details of people who died in the two World Wars has become far easier. The Commonwealth War Graves Commission published all its records on the Internet in November 1998. This includes the Debt of Honour Register containing names and details of 1.78 million casualties. Even with scant details it is possible to trace people. Each name called up has the rank, company, date and place of death. Further information gives a description of the battle, the circumstances and whatever else is known about the soldier and his regiment. Internet address: http://www.cwgc.org

For research into the casualties of other battles you may need a little more help; the Imperial War Museum might be able to advise you how to proceed.

Trade directories

Sometime in the eighteenth century these commercial directories began. They spread to most large towns and cities during the nineteenth century. The directories are useful because they begin with a short description of the area – information like population, names of large landowners, details of postal services, market days, innkeepers etc. They go on to list the various professional people, tradespeople and often local residents.

Even if you have traced someone on a census, there are 10 years in which you have no reference to them until the next census. This is where a trade or street directory can come in useful. Sometimes they let you down by listing only the middle class inhabitants, lesser mortals not appearing.

Tithe maps

These may be worth consulting for someone resident in the mid-nineteenth century when most parishioners had to pay a tenth of their income to the tithe owner, frequently the parish priest. Between 1836 and 1852 the tithe commissioners were sent out to every hamlet, parish and township to draw up maps of land ownership so that a charge could be fixed. Most of these maps still exist and, when read alongside the apportionment book, can yield useful information like the occupant, the landowner and the size of the plot of land involved. Old names of fields may well appear on the map as well. Approach the county record office to view tithe maps.

Rate books

Dating from the mid-eighteenth century, these can be another source of information about where people lived. As in the case of the tithe map, the county record office is the best place to look.

Types of family

Important local families

Researching significant families is always easier than humble ones. For one thing everybody has heard of them, locally if not nationally. The local library or county record office may hold family papers from the past, or know where they are held. Eminent families may also have a coat of arms which can be researched through the College of Arms.

Humble local families

Whilst the humble families may not have their coat of arms, a local history society or family history group could well have some information about them. If it is your lucky day, somebody may have done the research for you already! Well there's always hope! The village school may have surviving records from late Victorian times and some modern-day pupils may have been set projects connected with them – though perhaps that is pushing your luck too much.

In summary

As I said at the outset of this chapter, I have covered only a fraction of the range of documents you might consult. Even these sound formidable, but do not be put off. There are lots of very helpful people in public record offices and libraries who deal with novice researchers all the time. As you work through your research, ideas about the sort of thing you need to know will become apparent. Then you can begin to ask around. Someone *will* know where the records of a particular regiment are held. Be prepared for the frustration of tracking down the records you want, only to find that the particular year you require was lost in the flood/never recorded because of the war/has gone to be rebound. It does happen.

TRY THIS
- Study a birth certificate (not your own) and see how much information you can extract from it.
- Study an entry from the census then try writing up an account of that family using the material.

7 | COLLECTING ILLUSTRATIONS

Do you need illustrations?

When you begin your research you may not know whether you will be able to include pictures in your book. If you are planning to publish the work yourself, it will be down to what you can afford (pictures are more expensive to reproduce than text).

Even so, you *do* need to collect illustrations as you work. If you don't require them for publication, they will help with the writing. You will be able to paint a picture in words that tells the reader what someone looked like, perhaps explaining the character's fatal attraction to women!

What pictures do you want?

People

You will want to collect as many pictures of your subject as you can, unless that person is someone like a pop star or the late Princess of Wales, in which case pictures abound. In all cases a few images from different stages of their life are helpful. You may want pictures to demonstrate a specific point about the person. If your subject lived a long time ago, you will probably be grateful for every picture that comes your way.

Photography began around 1840 and the earliest photographs are called daguerreotypes. These were printed on glass and can be hard to decipher, not just because they fade, but because you have to hold them in a certain way to catch the light. The image vanishes like a hologram or turns into a mirror at certain angles. For that reason they are notoriously difficult to copy and require specialist photography. However, because they are so early they are uncommon.

Early photographs of your subject may well be hard to come by. Much depends on the prosperity of the family. As the nineteenth century progressed, photography became an increasingly popular medium to record significant events in life, like marriage. Nevertheless, it is unlikely a poor family could have afforded even that.

With some subjects you might search for portrait paintings. Again it will depend on the wealth and status of the family. But don't assume that you are only looking for Gainsborough or Burne-Jones portraits of your subject. There were plenty of lesser-known portrait painters who travelled round the country recording the likenesses of gentleman farmers and their ladies to adorn their drawing room walls. Such paintings tend to remain in the family. Young girls from the middle classes were encouraged to sketch and paint – a suitably lady-like pastime – and their efforts may survive amongst family papers.

If your subject was famous, the National Portrait Gallery in the UK and the USA is an excellent place to look for pictures, both painted and photographic. Their published catalogue is available in many reference libraries, but it is not exhaustive. It is advisable to write and check their current holdings.

Don't restrict your search to images of your subject. You also need to collect pictures of their family, friends and associates. Perhaps your subject met someone like Oscar Wilde or President Johnson during their career. It might be appropriate to include a picture of the celebrity as he or she looked then. It certainly helps to have a photocopy of that celebrity by you, so you can comment on the facial features that would have caught your subject's attention – things like thinning hair or hooded eyes. The inclusion of such detail helps the reader identify with the subject and to visualize this meeting you are writing about.

Places

Pictures of places will give variety to the illustrations in the finished book and the reader will want to know what the house or village looked like when the subject lived there. Keep your eyes open for old postcards of relevant places. They can often be purchased cheaply at antique fairs and junk shops.

Again use these illustrations to help you to paint a picture in words. The photograph of the house where your subject grew up may show large trees at the side or a sweeping drive in front. You might be able to describe this from a child's point of view.

Don't forget that before photographs there were engravings and, going forward in time, you could look for newspaper pictures, film or video.

All these photographs could be expensive, if you include everything you find. However, some you want in your book and some you just want to work from. Try to photocopy most of the illustrations which might be of use later. It is easy to photocopy pages from books and sections of newspaper and even old photographs. They don't come out terribly well, but all you require is a copy in your file to refer to. Later you can show a publisher what is available, so that pictures for the finished book can be selected.

As with all research, record the details as you go. On the back of your photocopy or picture, write down where you saw the illustration – name of the library, the book, catalogue number, page number etc. What information was written about the picture? What date was it? Who owns the picture? Any copyright information? In fact, absolutely anything which might help you to order a copy of that picture over the phone. If the information is going on the back of a photograph, write the details on a sticky label first. This prevents the pressure of the pen or pencil wrecking the picture.

If one of your interviewees possesses a photograph you want, see if they will let you run down to the local newsagent or petrol station to photocopy it. If that is out of the question, try and photograph it yourself. Prop it up on a cushion and snap away: all you need is a record of what exists. I've got many photographs taken on my idiot-proof camera (point and snap). One is of a little sepia photograph next to the jam dish, on a tea trolley in someone's sitting room. Although the picture in question is small and the paraphernalia of tea is much in evidence, it was enough for the publisher to agree that it was ideal for the dust jacket, and they later sent their own photographer to do a proper job.

Maps

You may not need maps to illustrate your biography, but they are useful to have as you write. How else would you know what was within walking distance of the subject's house, or down the road? In some cases a map will be an essential tool, say if your subject's career was intimately bound up with the landscape in terms of natural history or perhaps archaeology. Once again, maps enable you to bring things to life by providing a description of the landscape.

You can usually locate maps in large public libraries or county archives. Parts can often be photocopied for study purposes, provided the section copied is only a small portion of the whole. A photocopy is particularly useful because you can get your felt pens out and colour rivers, boundaries and key buildings, all of which makes the map more useful to you at a quick glance.

Maybe your completed biography will require a map to show your subject's activities in the area. If so, the publisher can use the various maps you have assembled to commission one specifically for the book.

I have dwelt on county libraries and archives as useful sources of illustrations but there are of course national archives, picture agencies and specialist sources of illustrations. Some of the major museums, auction houses, university libraries and provincial art galleries can supply illustrations for publication. Obtaining illustrations from these institutions can prove expensive. There will be a loan fee for the transparency and a reproduction fee payable. If that is the only source of a picture, it may be worth the cost. However, paying for illustrations may well be the responsibility of the publisher. It depends on your contract.

It is impossible to list all the different types of organization that could supply pictures. You can get free advice from public libraries about places to try. And once again it is worth checking the acknowledgements in published books connected with the subject to see where illustrations came from.

TRY THIS

- Write a 100-word description of someone from a Victorian photograph.
- Using a section from a map, write a description of a walk between two places incorporating features you have seen on the map.

8 | PLACES

Try to go there

Houses

It is worth trying to visit all the locations associated with your subject. This may be impossible if the place is abroad or at the opposite end of the country, but go wherever you can. You soon realize how helpful it can be when you have read about a house first, then visit it. Somehow it's never quite what you expected. Either the house is much larger than you thought, or more drab. You also get a feel of the area when you are actually standing there. Perhaps you realize how hemmed in it must have seemed to the occupants after their previous house or how impossibly steep the back garden was for the disabled woman. Visits help you to avoid stupid errors and stereotyping. It is easy to state glibly that such-and-such a town was grim, when a visit shows there were outstanding views of the mountains all around. Conversely the seemingly idyllic village might turn out to be bleak and windswept or overshadowed by large slag heaps.

It can happen that you track down a location, only to discover that the house has been demolished. Sometimes, although the house exists, you may not be able to go inside because it is private property and the present owners do not welcome researchers snooping round. Even so a visit to the area is still worthwhile. Only by going there do you understand how breathtaking the views over the river are. Or that the coal measures are so close to the surface that the soil is black and the vegetation is sparse.

Houses can survive unexpectedly. I tracked down the house which was home to George Eliot for the first 21 years of her life and found it transformed into a Beefeater restaurant. No problems gaining access this time. Indeed, I had a drink in her father's study, now renamed the Snug Bar! You could still see the original flagstones on the floor and the sash windows that looked out up the old driveway. If I closed my ears to the bleeps and clatter as the one-armed bandit spewed out coins, it was possible to imagine a little of life there in the 1830s.

Try photographing the properties you visit and the surrounding area. These are not pictures for publication, unless you are a real whiz with the camera. They are just to have by you when you are working on the relevant chapters.

Towns and villages

Just as useful are visits to the villages or the relevant parts of a town where your subject lived or worked. The village will probably have expanded, but it is a fairly safe bet that the area round the church will be largely untouched. Your subject may not have been religious, indeed might have had a real aversion to religion, but they probably knew this part of the village well from attending family events there.

The original streets and roads are still likely to be there, even if the buildings either side have changed dramatically. What tends to happen is that new roads get added, rather than old ones moved. Pubs also tend to be survivors. So stop off: call in to see if they have any old pictures, maps or memorabilia adorning their walls. Do they know anything about the old days?

Churches

Churches are similarly worth a visit. They may have preserved material from the period you are interested in. It can be worth paying for the church guidebook or a few postcards for future reference. A walk round the churchyard is always worthwhile. There might be a monument to a family who dominated local life during your subject's time. On a tombstone you might read of a major local disaster, like a mine explosion or ship-wreck, that coincided with your subject's life in the area. This is something you could follow up later to give a flavour of the period.

Look at everything. Church and village notice boards are worth a glance. I note down names and phone numbers of churchwardens, vicars and village hall officials in case I am desperate for a contact to chase something up later. A conversation with the church brass cleaners once proved invaluable and led me to a descendant of my subject! Similarly, a chat with someone in the local pub might put you on the trail of an amateur historian or an elderly resident with a good memory.

Fill in the background

To get the most out of a visit, read up on the area beforehand. Failing that, call at the local newsagent or village shop to see if they have a guidebook. These humble publications, produced on someone's kitchen table and photocopied at the local primary school in aid of the village preservation society, are not to be scorned. They may be the only source of information.

If there is a school in the area, you could write to enquire whether any of the pupils have ever done a local survey that you might read. Check the local studies department of the library to see if they have copies of any older guide books that have been produced or even a limited edition Victorian rector's history of the village. Fortunately, most Tourist Information Centres focus on local heritage, so pick up their leaflets and buy their guide book to assist in your research. And whilst you are there, don't forget maps. Even a modern map is useful and the larger the scale the better. You might need to identify the marshy bits or old battlefields!

Write to the nearest museum ahead of your trip, telling them who you are researching. They may be worth a visit too. I've never forgotten one provincial museum that produced a shoe box of unsorted material, deposited by an associate of my subject. The box was listed in their inventory, but had been put away in a store cupboard and forgotten about. It was a little goldmine of letters, photographs and scraps of paper. This is where the mobile biographer has the advantage over the person who does his or her research from their study, doesn't plod the streets, probe the dusty corners or chat to the bloke pinning up the parish council notices.

Yes, it is time-consuming and it has to be fitted in when you have the opportunity, not necessarily when your research reaches that point. But it's fun. My visits have taken me to places I'd never have visited and have even dictated venues for family holidays. A week in Bedfordshire may not sound as glamorous as a week in Tuscany,

I admit, but it has been enjoyable with houses to hunt for, information to check and illustrations to unearth.

When you can't go there

Don't lose heart if you can't possibly go to the area. Other people have probably been and written about it. There was no way I could have followed Alice Kipling (mother of Rudyard) to India, so I read various accounts of Bombay and Lahore written by nineteenth-century travellers. It worked. I took heart from H.R.F. Keating who said that he had written his early Inspector Ghote novels, which deal with the exploits of an Inspector of the Bombay Police, without ever visiting the subcontinent. His secret was careful use of maps, guide books and other people's eyes.

A useful address

The National Monuments Record Centre, Kemble Drive, Swindon, Wiltshire, SN2 2GZ has a large archive which includes 3 million photographs of buildings. This may be useful if the property you are searching for has been demolished. Their archive also includes aerial photographs of most of England and a Listed Building Information Service. The National Monument Record has a separate centre for buildings in London and can be contacted at 55, Blandford Street, London, W1H 3AF. It is possible to arrange visits in person to both places or to pay for a search to be done on your behalf.

Aerial photographic surveys in the US are more fragmented. The main organizations involved in the US are the National Park Services and some anthropology departments of universities, so it would be worth starting research with them. The British journal *Aerial Archaeology* (published by Aerial Archaeology Foundation) issue 1979/1980 devoted a whole issue to US aerial photography.

TRY THIS

- ■ Try to locate some written accounts of life in a distant country during the past. Read these for background research.
- ■ Write a short account of some aspect you have found out about.

---

9 PRIMARY SOURCES

What are primary sources?

These are the most important tools of the biographer because they are the first-hand accounts of what people actually said or wrote. The best primary source, of course, is an interview with the subject: *you* can put questions, hear the replies and ask further.

If a face-to-face interview is out of the question, the subject's writings, or recordings of them talking, are valuable primary sources because no one is interpreting for you. You need the first-hand accounts to judge for yourself, in the light of your research, what was going through the person's mind. As always in biography writing, you are trying to get under the skin of the main character. You want to know what made them tick.

The danger of reading only secondary accounts (*someone else's* comments on the evidence) is that you may not agree with the author's interpretations. Your research may have led you to understand the subject's quirky humour, so you know that some of their comments are not to be taken literally. Or that they regularly dashed off letters in a temper and regretted them instantly, so a particular vitriolic diatribe was not as serious as it sounded. One source may say that X was deeply in love with Y, a judgement the biographer based on the reading of one letter. However, you may have read many similar letters and have realized that the subject always wrote in this way to his girlfriends, so these words are no proof of deep love.

Examples of primary sources

Letters

On the subject of letters, where do you find them? Well, like the hunt for the descendants, it can be a painstaking business. It is possible many were destroyed, but it is rare for every single one to have been thrown out. The first thing to bear in mind is that letters are likely to be with the *recipient*, rather than the author. So you need to be looking for *their* papers. If they were famous, follow the same procedure as you did in the hunt for the descendants – check the back of biographies or books associated with their period, locality or discipline. If they were not famous, the quarry can be more elusive.

Papers tend to be deposited in archives near the family home, or possibly in university libraries associated with the subject's discipline. There is always the huge British Library holding. You might write asking if they have papers relating to your subject. At the same time you can request a form to apply for a reader's ticket.

Libraries and archives can be notoriously long in replying. I recall waiting six months for one university library to answer my enquiry (that's my record and I don't want to beat it) and then I had to apply again for copies of what I wanted to see. This can be incredibly frustrating if you are waiting desperately for particular information in order to proceed.

It is equally frustrating to discover that the papers have been sold to archives abroad. I know that it's our fault: when the papers came up for sale years ago no one was interested. Fortunately, there were buyers somewhere who could conserve them in modern archives. Actually most libraries and archives are very helpful and can arrange for researchers to obtain the cheapest copies for study. I have been sent photocopies and even reels of microfilm to work from. The latter was not ideal, but when hundreds of letters were involved, photocopying was impossible and a visit to Yale too expensive, microfilm was the only answer. When I explained the problem to the local library, they let me use one of their microfiche readers for a few hours at a time (believe me that is all you can handle – it makes you go cross-eyed). Then you've got to sit and make notes from the letters. Because my trips were limited, I got into the habit of taking a pocket tape recorder and quietly (don't get yourself thrown out) reading aloud each letter on to tape (say the punctuation as you go in case you ever need to quote it). I got through the material fairly quickly that way, then transcribed what I needed at home.

Diaries

These are probably the most useful primary source because they are the nearest thing to the person's thoughts at that time. But diaries vary. You have only got to compare your own (if you keep one) with Samuel Pepys's or even Adrian Mole's! Some can be a list of appointments, others an intimate record of the writer's thoughts and feelings.

Also, it is worth asking *why* the person kept a diary in the first place. Was it intended as an aide-memoir? That would explain the list of appointments with no evaluation of their use. If the diary was kept with a view to publishing at a later date, perhaps to boost the pension fund and settle a few old scores, the biographer needs to keep that in mind. We all hope to stumble upon the private diary which was a debate with the soul and never intended to be read by anyone else, let alone for publication.

Diaries are not necessarily *complete* records. I remember happily working through the personal diaries of my subject's mother until I was pulled up short by one entry. It read, 'Woke up feeling a little unwell this morning. Gave birth to a daughter at 5am.' She hadn't even mentioned that she was pregnant! Another of her tantalising entries read: 'Events today too terrible to write here.' It suddenly struck me that she *knew* someone else was going to read this diary. It makes you wonder what else you are not being told.

Autobiography

This is a valuable primary source because it gives the author's view of events and people, with the benefit of hindsight. In many ways the autobiography is a variant on the published diary. It's worth remembering that the author's view may not be the same perception that everyone had of those particular events and could even be a rose-coloured vision of things. But even taken as a partial view of a life and events, autobiographies are still extremely valuable and sometimes the only account you can find.

Do you believe all you read?

In a nutshell, no. Why should a person be any more honest in writing than they would be in person? It depends, of course, on what you know of your subject's personality and the reasons you think the letter, diary or autobiography was written.

Things like private jokes, throw-away lines and topical humour can be almost impossible to understand or even identify 50 years later. So, although a person wasn't writing lies, they may not have intended their remark to be taken at face value and the recipient would have known that too. The intended audience, if any, for a diary will affect how much credence you give to the account. Maybe the diary contains the author's first impression of a situation, but later they changed their mind. As an account of what they thought *at the time* it is of great value.

Think about the reasons why people write letters. The letter to an insurance company explaining how the chimney pot came down in high winds, broke every tile in its passage and then destroyed the greenhouse may not be an accurate account of the events that night. Similarly the letter written to a lover breaking off an affair may not give the true reasons. Letters written by children to their parents may contain information that the child thinks is good for the parent to hear. The fact that some major catastrophe is not mentioned doesn't mean the writer was unaware of it.

Yes it's all very devious, but people are. Your subject is, or was, a real, breathing person with all the foibles and weaknesses that make us human.

A final point of caution is not to invest too much significance in a single letter. Its survival could be due to chance and it may not be truly representative of the person. If the only letter that survived from your childhood was the one you wrote in class and passed round whilst the teacher was writing on the board, what would it reveal about you? That you had a mind like a sewer? That you were totally stupid?

TRY THIS

- Read and compare entries from a published diary like *The Diary of Anne Frank* with that of a political figure.
- How close to the real subject do you feel you get in these diaries?

10 | SECONDARY SOURCES

What are secondary sources?

These are the accounts someone else wrote about your subject or an event connected with them. This account is not necessarily what your subject said or thought, but is an *interpretation* by a third party and as such will be coloured by their views. That does not mean secondary sources are no use. Far from it, they are valuable simply because they reflect what other people thought about a certain issue at the time of writing.

It is especially useful to read what *contemporaries* said about your subject. Also read what later writers thought and how they evaluated those same activities.

Views can vary tremendously over time. The role and achievements of women is one significant area where attitudes have changed. Another is a person's private life. Attitudes towards sexuality have changed over the years. It is not just that there is a greater degree of sexual tolerance, there is also an increased interest in the subject. What was *not* said in an earlier account can be as revealing as what *was* said.

Examples of secondary sources

Other authors' biographies of the subject

It is worth reading some of them, but bear in mind that they may colour your judgement. One of the significant things you have to offer as a biographer is that you have read the primary sources and can offer a new interpretation. Once you know that someone else judged an episode as indicative of your subject's meanness, it can be terribly hard to approach the incident with an open mind. So whilst other biographies are useful, it might be better to look at them *after* you have done most of your work on the subject.

Autobiographies

Look wide when considering secondary sources. Obviously you need to read what friends said about your subject but the opinions of opponents, even enemies, are valuable if you are to create a rounded picture. From these accounts you can see whether the subject was regarded as revolutionary, controversial or simply ignored as a crank. The autobiographies of contemporaries who knew your subject may be worth investigating for these slants. Such writings give a flavour of the social scene, the period or the country, offering valuable details which you can incorporate into your writing.

Newspapers

Contemporary newspapers may be worth reading. Local papers can be particularly helpful and are often available at a library in the area. Obituaries in local newspapers can yield addresses and solve family relationships. The mourners at a funeral may be listed in detail in a local paper, which can provide valuable clues in the hunt for descendants.

Obituaries are well worth checking at both national and local level. Different writers will address their report to their particular audience. Hence an obituary in a medical journal will concentrate on the subject's academic and surgical achievements, whereas a local paper may mention that the church choir will miss his excellent tenor voice and that he is a great loss to the world of dobermann breeding. You need to read both accounts if you are to understand the man, although you may subsequently only use some of the information in your biography.

TRY THIS
- Look at the bibliography of a published biography and spot which primary and which secondary sources have been used.

11 | COMPLETING YOUR RESEARCH

How do you know when you have finished your research?

The simple answer to this question is that you can never finish your research. Not very helpful I know, but there never is a point when you have been into everything you could ever research. There will always be another angle you could try, another place you might visit or another information search you could instigate. Research is like a still pool into which you have thrown a pebble. The ripples continue outwards in concentric circles forever. It is worth noticing that the ripples become less conspicuous as they get further and further from the centre of the action.

Rule off

Realistically, you have to decide when to draw a line under your research, a time when you have followed up all the *obvious* leads and should think about writing the material up. It is possible that something will turn up after you have finished researching, but that should not necessitate a total recasting of your argument because you formed your opinions from a *wide range* of material. I suppose the worst scenario is that a cache of letters turns up showing your subject had a secret affair with a woman who was the muse for his greatest opus. Then, I guess, it would be back to basics. You might not consider this the worst case scenario: it is the best possible reason for having to do lots more work. After all no one else has seen this new material. You have all the aces in your hand!

When do you start writing?

It is probably best to begin your writing once you have got a reasonable amount of the early research done, then continue the research alongside the writing. Once you start writing, your brain will tease away at things, start turning things over and raising questions. This, in turn, will suggest further research or even a source of information you had not considered before. For instance, you might be working on your subject's middle years, when a friend from their childhood pops up. This offers new openings for research and, possibly, a new slant on their early life. It is not a problem, you can always go back to the early chapters to integrate new material. This is one of the great advantages of using a word processor for your writings.

In practice, you never stop researching until you've written the last word of the last chapter. Often, it is only by working through a chapter or a period of the subject's life that you discover what you need to know about. And because information doesn't come in at times convenient to the writing, research and writing have to go along together. I suppose it must be very similar to filming – the producer shoots sections out of sequence because it makes geographic and economic sense to do so. Then, at the end, the film is edited into the right order and it all joins together beautifully.

There are other advantages to researching and writing as you go. Sometimes a marvellous source of information comes in which you are just itching to write about. I remember being really fired up by a collection of letters written by Alice Kipling, mother of Rudyard, soon after she had arrived in India. They were wonderful because she was so candid about the snobbishness of people in society and her own misery in that alien country. After I had read them I knew exactly how she felt and I was just dying to weave them together into a story, so I did. The writing was all the more vivid because of my enthusiasm at that time.

Later I was able to slot the section into the relevant part of the book, making a few additions and subtractions so that it sat comfortably.

At other times you might be getting bogged down with a chapter that you are writing and feel you can't see the wood for the trees. That is when it can be sheer bliss to go off to a library to read some letters or visit one of the subject's relatives to do an interview. A change of tasks also has the advantage of getting the brain going again for further writing.

Part Two –
WRITING

12 | YOUR READER

Think about your audience

This is enormously important and, whilst you may not have considered the reader consciously, you probably have some idea at the back of your mind of the type of person you are writing for. There's no snobbery attached to this; it's not better to write for one type of person than for another. Everyone is a potential reader, from a six-year-old to a 90-year-old. Within that large age range there is also an enormous variety of interest groups.

The perfect present

Writers often forget that books are given as presents, especially biographies. So it is worth remembering that your reader may not have chosen your book for themselves. People might think of your book as the perfect present for Aunty Flo or young Gary. Indeed, it is very flattering that people are confident that *your book* will give pleasure to others. Biographies are often preferred to novels as presents because purchasers think that they are unlikely to cause offence, whereas a novel chosen inadvertently for Aunty Flo may contain some very steamy scenes on page 63! Buying a novel for someone is rather like choosing their clothes: it only works if you know the person well. A biography, however, has human interest and everyone is interested in people. It's not just illustrated biographies, the so-called 'coffee-table books', that are given as presents. You have only to look through the list of best-sellers or at Christmas window displays in bookshops to see what appeals.

Why does the reader matter?

It sounds obvious, but the reader is going to *read* your book. This means that they may be selecting it from the shelf in the library, purchasing it in the bookshop or unwrapping it as a gift. Some readers are going to part with their hard-earned cash to buy your book and, hence, determine its success or failure. All readers will have expectations of your biography which *you* need to meet, if the book is to succeed for them. You may think, 'I can't please everybody' but you've got to try!

You need to have an idea of what your reader is seeking from your biography. It will determine your approach, the planning, the detail, the references, your voice - in short the whole way in which you tackle the book.

Spotting your reader

The child

It's worth remembering that children are readers too and they like stories about people's lives as well. Too often the would-be biographer forgets that this important market exists. Chapter 24 looks at writing for children.

The subject boff

This species is only interested in one particular field of study, be it jazz, the eighteenth century, railways, native Americans or whatever. This means they read everything connected with the subject, belong to the society and know a great deal about the background to your biography. Don't be scared! If you have done your research carefully and can substantiate everything you have written, there is no problem. Quite the opposite. You have tapped into a ready and keen market for books about your subject. Hopefully, you have added to that field of study.

These readers are also likely to write to you, via the publisher, after publication, to add to your knowledge, correct or challenge something you have said or simply tell you how much they have enjoyed the book. It always nice to receive the praise, you get a warm glow inside for a while. The other sorts of letters can be interesting – even the ones that tell you you've got it wrong are useful. We all get them. No matter how carefully you did your research, there may some information you never looked at or didn't have access to. Fine. Acknowledge the correction gratefully and plan to incorporate it into a later edition.

The biography-reader

This sort of reader complements the previous category. The biography-reader doesn't mind what field your subject excelled in, provided it is a true story. These readers prefer reading biography to fiction, which they consider to be a waste of time, because it never happened. Now this reader may have a limited knowledge of military campaigns, the cinema or missionary work in Africa, but they have a vast general knowledge accumulated from reading biographies over the years. Incidentally, they are ideal people to have in your team on Quiz Night at the village hall or down the pub!

What interests this reader is the *humanity* of the subject. They really want to get under the skin of the subject and understand their reactions to the different events in their life. This reader is less concerned about references and notes at the back of the book; they probably will not give them a second glance because they trust you, the writer, to have done the research carefully.

The academic

Some would-be biographers assume these people are going to be the main readers of their book. This is probably not the case. Since their use of biography is for work rather than pleasure, it is quite likely that the academic will not read your biography from cover to cover at all. In much the same way as you used books for research, they may consult the index to locate the information they want. Your beautiful turns of phrase or gentle touches of humour may go unread and unappreciated, whereas the notes and references, as well as the bibliography (and possibly the acknowledgements), will be well-used and appreciated. The academic expects accuracy of research and copious notes to support all the points or suppositions that are made.

The man or woman in the street

It is a wide street and all humanity passes. What this reader most requires is a good page-turner. They may have chosen your book because of a favourable review, a friend's recommendation, a prominent window display or they just liked the cover. This reader wants to be entertained. They consume a wide variety of material including magazines and novels, but have chosen a biography on this occasion because they want a true story to read.

They require that you tell a good yarn, engage their interest and make them turn the page – not the sort of book once described as 'hard to pick up once you've put it down'! In all likelihood, this reader will not give your notes and references a glance but will enjoy the human-interest factor of the book. With them in mind, you need to consider the issue of biography as an art-form, half-way between history and fiction (see page vi).

It is possible to go on attempting to define other sorts of readers, but these examples should be enough to get you thinking about who is most likely to form the main audience for your book. Naturally, there will be elements of all types in the readership, but you probably have one group in mind more than the others. Consider what implications that has for the way you tackle the subject, from planning to writing.

TRY THIS
- Pick up several different biographies and try to decide what sort of reader was in the writer's mind.
- What sort of group would you want to write for?

13 | WHAT HAVE YOU GOT TO SAY ABOUT YOUR SUBJECT?

Focus your mind

This might seem a silly question to ask but you need to know the answer to shape your forthcoming biography. It is certainly a question I ask myself at the outset, then again when I'm planning the chapters and I try to keep it in mind during the writing. The reason is that the answer to this question stops me waffling! It is quite a simple technique to focus the mind. It can also prevent you from writing a biography of a famous person that is exactly like the previous biographies about them.

Once you have made up your mind about what you want to say, you will be able to select the best material confidently. You may have discovered the great man's original air ticket during the course of your research and found it intriguing, but, if you are brutally honest with yourself, the document does not advance anyone's understanding of the subject one iota. I have always found a diary provides the biggest temptation to deviate from the main argument. It's always full of fascinating period details, but they don't all have to be included just because I know them.

What you say depends on when you say it!

The first biography of the subject

If your biography is the first one to be written about this person, the question about what you have to say is easily answered. You have got everything to say about your subject. Your aim may be to give a fully rounded picture of the subject and to celebrate their achievements. Or, depending on your intended audience, you may have decided that the main thrust of this biography is the subject's achievements and their importance in a particular field, whilst their personality and character will only be touched on.

You are not the first

What if your biography is by no means the first to be written about this person? The question 'What have *you* got to say about your subject?' is even more pertinent. And if you don't ask it, a potential publisher certainly will! The answer may be that you have discovered a series of letters or have stumbled on a hitherto unknown piece of work by your subject. This would certainly constitute a reason for a reappraisal of the life. Whilst the archives for a topic may have been raked over many times, it is always possible that you appear on the scene at the time an heir dies, or just as a 100-year bar is lifted, so that new papers suddenly enter the public domain.

It is also possible that you may want to reinterpret the life. You might feel that previous biographies were too reverential, creating an unreal portrait by lauding the virtues and ignoring the vices.

It was certainly the opportunity to reinterpret a life which persuaded me to accept a commission to write a biography of George Eliot. Knowing that the archives had been well and truly trawled, it was unlikely that I would come up with a hoard of letters, but new light on her character was required. My examination of the official biography instantly showed the scope for a new interpretation. I found the author was a male American professor of literature who had set out to interpret the life in terms of the writings, making one mirror the other wherever possible. I, on the other hand, was a woman with a particular fascination for the way George Eliot had managed to lead such a daring life in mid-Victorian society and get away with it. Added to that, I noticed that most of George Eliot's biographers had covered the half of her life spent in the Midlands in a chapter or two, preferring to devote most of the book to her 30 in London after she became famous. I couldn't help thinking that these first 30 years in provincial obscurity might well hold the key to understanding the woman. This was definitely a new approach, and answered the question about what *I* wanted to say about this subject.

If your subject is alive

This is always a difficult area because what you *want* to say and what you *can* say might be different. If you have agreed to write the authorized biography, it will be with the subject's co-operation. What you have got to say about your subject is very much what *they want* to say, whether you believe it to be the truth or not. You have no more freedom to make up your own mind about situations or people than if you were ghosting an autobiography.

If you choose to write about a young, modern-day personality, it can be very difficult to make an accurate judgement about the significance of their life. The 18-year-old football hero who has risen to fame very rapidly and seems destined for stardom has had a very brief life so far. It is very difficult to view this life in perspective. In a case like this, what you have to say about the life will be shaped by your intended readership. In the case of the footballer, you are likely to be writing for a largely teenage audience, so it would be wise to select your material and develop your argument to appeal to their particular interests.

If your subject doesn't want you to say anything

The unauthorized biography is quite another matter. You have certainly got the freedom to make up your own mind about situations and people, but the spectre of libel action may shape your judgement. As we have seen, the authorized biography can be one-sided, since everything is seen through the subject's eyes. The same concern exists with the unauthorized biography since the story is gleaned only from those who will talk. These may be friends of the subject or, if the subject has made it known that they don't want a biography, you may only get the viewpoint of those who have scores to settle.

TRY THIS
- Consider what new approach you might take if you were writing a biography of Queen Victoria.
- How would you tackle a biography of a popular girl band?

14 | PLANNING YOUR BOOK

Biography does not write itself

Unlike a novel and in line with most forms of non-fiction writing, biography does need a *structure*. One of the joys of reading biography is seeing how one experience in a person's life leads on to another, or how a certain relationship develops. This only happens in a book because the author has contrived it. Without that careful selection of the relevant and omission of irrelevant material, the book would mirror life too closely – everything would be muddled together and you would not be able to see the wood for the trees.

When do you start planning?

You start planning the book right from the outset, even though you have barely started the research. You probably had a vague idea when you chose the subject which parts of the life were interesting and would form the core of your book. In addition, you need some information about where the person came from and what happened to them after their moment(s) of glory. You can allocate pages very roughly from this starting point.

Devising a structure

Divide the life up

A simple structure is to divide the life into manageable chunks, perhaps:

- The start
- The middle
- The end.

The start

At this point, it is helpful to turn to your timeline (see page 19) to help you divide the life up. Even though you may know comparatively little about the early life, you could allocate a chapter to it, possibly two. In addition, you will probably want to make some reference to the subject's forebears in order to set them in context. The reader will need an understanding of the family background in terms of wealth, interests and geographical location. It is worth planning to cover this area to some extent. A couple of pages may suffice, if there appears to be no obvious link between the activities of the ancestors and the achievements of the hero or heroine. I certainly would not recommend ploughing through the lives of the great-grandparents, the grandparents and the parents just because I had the information. This would be tedious for the reader itching to meet the main character. So, allocate a couple of pages to the ancestors initially, it is simple enough to expand this into a full chapter if necessary.

The end

If you aren't sure of the details of the whole life at the time of your initial planning, that's no problem. From the beginning of the life move directly to the end. You will need to cover the death of your subject, but do you actually want that to be the end of the book? Would it be helpful to have a chapter evaluating their achievements, considering what happened to their popularity after their death or looking at the progress of their descendants? None of these are *necessary*: you decide as you plan. Chapter 28 considers endings in more detail but at this stage sketch in a rough ending.

The middle

So with the beginning and the end in place, you can turn your attention to the middle. The easiest part to put in next is the famous bit and you may feel this warrants several chapters, even though it represents a very short time chronologically. That's fine. As a rule of thumb, give each event the same prominence in the book as it had in the life.

Against the chapters you have already decided on, write in brackets the years you expect to cover, say (1836-40) or even (May 1835). Again, your timeline will come in handy here.

Planning the rest of the book is going to be a matter of inspired guesswork at this early stage. But that doesn't matter. A flexible plan is far better than no plan at all. Without a plan you may discover that you have wasted your time writing a whole chapter about the subject's school days just because you happened to discover an old exercise book. Later much of the chapter may have to be dumped because it distorts the overall book.

If I really don't know anything about the rest of the life but have got the birth, death and famous bit sketched in, I'd provisionally settle for dividing the rest of the life up into handy parcels. Depending how long they lived, I might choose to allocate a chapter a decade. I might do this chronologically through time (say one chapter for 1850 to 1860) or perhaps more usefully deal with the subject's twenties then their thirties. It's very rough and ready, I know, but at least there is some framework to hang the writing on. If you are not sure how you are going to tackle one particularly complicated part of the life, where lots of things happen simultaneously, don't agonize over it. Just put down a few scribbled ideas, albeit weak ones, then move on. Things will become clearer later. It's amazing how sections work out when you get there. With the outline in place you are ready to start writing.

How many chapters do you have and how long are they?

There is not a correct answer to either part of the question. As much as anything, be guided by your intended reader. Children tend to have a shorter concentration span, so avoid a long book and long chapters. No insult to the man or woman in the street, but they probably prefer shorter chapters to long ones (over 5,000 words can be hard going). If the book is being read for entertainment, it may be picked up and put down at odd times. Shorter chapters are more convenient for occasional reading. The reader feels they are not losing the gist of the argument.

Another possible tip is to look at biographies that you have admired and would like to emulate. If you are completely in the dark, then experiment with 10 or 12 chapters to see if you can accommodate the proposed material. When you do begin working, the precise number will become clear. Unless you are superstitious, any number is the correct one. As to the length of your chapters, see how a specimen chapter pans out. Chapters don't all have to be the same length. Indeed you may feel that a particular chapter works better divided into two shorter ones, rather than the planned longer one. Trust your gut feeling, not word counts.

Shrinking and expanding

Don't worry if the chronology is not equally spaced out in terms of chapters. In fact, I'd worry more if it was all neatly worked out into equal parcels of years! Your biography should reflect the high and low points of the life not simply the passage of time.

As you continue to research and, more significantly, to write, you will be thinking the material through. The exact nature of the chapters will become clear. An area that you had previously known little about may suddenly take on a special significance and demand more extensive treatment. Others to which you had allocated a whole chapter, may later prove inconsequential and shrink. But either way if a general framework of chapters exists, you know where your high point is going to be as you write. Keeping that focus as you progress makes for a tight structure to the biography.

TRY THIS

■ Make a provisional 10 chapter plan for your subject, particularly considering how you will apportion the middle chapters in the book.

---

15 | STARTING TO WRITE

Where does the book begin?

At the beginning might seem the obvious answer. In practice, the beginning can be the hardest place to start. Are we talking about the beginning of the book or the beginning of the subject's life? And are they the same anyway? This is not meant to be a conundrum.

Some authors choose to start their biographies with the subject well and truly born, indeed in action at a significant moment in their life. Then the early life is completed, in subsequent chapters, by flashback. This technique is not common and perhaps not advisable for a newcomer to biography writing, because it demands enormous skill in writing coupled with incredible manipulation of the material. I would also question whether such an approach is popular with the reader. I think the reader feels more comfortable with the natural logic of birth, life and death – a sequence which retains an element of suspense. How will she get her big break-through? Or will he succeed against these odds?

Putting pen to paper

Whatever you decide to have as your opening chapter, it doesn't have to be the one that you write first. Once you have done a reasonable amount of research you are probably itching to put pen to paper, or fingers to keyboard. The idea of plodding through the dusty ancestors may not be that appealing and may also seem to have little relevance to the life as you know it. That's fine. Leave it till later, even until last.

Start in the middle

There may be a section of research you have been working on recently that has really caught your imagination. Maybe you have read a wonderful account of an event which has enabled you to visualize exactly what was going on and what your subject thought about it all. Add to this some background reading about the place and the chief participants, and before long you are dying to dramatize that material into a chapter. So go ahead. Write that episode up even though you have not written any other part of the biography. It may later become part of chapter seven and drop into the final version with only minor adjustments. It is likely to be some of the most vivid writing, because you are all fired up with enthusiasm to write. And let's face it, biography is literature so good writing is what you are aiming for.

In general, I would not advise continuing to work out of sequence, unless you feel strongly that this method is right for you. There is a lot to be gained by working through events in the order that the subject experienced them. That way you are facing the same problems they did with the same background knowledge. As the biographer, you stand a greater chance of getting inside your subject's head when it comes to understanding their reactions.

There are, however, a few advantages in producing at least one chapter out of context. One is that you have got an interesting chapter to send to a potential publisher – more riveting reading than a trawl through the ancestors. But by far and away the best reason is that it makes you feel good! You have proved to yourself that you can write something worthwhile and you will be encouraged to write more. It's not just the beginner who needs that sense of achievement, everyone does. Each new subject is a fresh challenge and, until you start, you are not sure how you are going to settle into it and whether you can do it all. Positive feedback helps me a lot.

Start at the beginning

If, however, you do prefer to start writing at the beginning with the first chapter, don't agonize over it. It's not worth it. That might seem a flippant thing to say, but almost certainly the first chapter, possibly the first three, will have to be worked over again. Once you have got to the end of the book, you will have an overview of the life and will be able to identify which really were the significant points in the background or who were the influential ancestors. *Then* return to the first chapter and rearrange the material to support the point you are trying to make. Whilst it may involve a rewrite, it is probably not a huge undertaking. Most likely it will be a case of rearranging the material to stress the case you are making.

You may decide to drop most of the information about the grandfather in favour of a description of the mental illness that beset your subject's uncle, now that you can see a link with the problems that bedevilled the subject's middle years. Discussing this in chapter one will enable you to refer back later, thus keeping a tight grip on the structure of the biography.

Finally, that elusive opening sentence of the book, which in the past you spent a day writing, crossing out and rewriting, becomes apparent. Previous efforts are dumped in favour of something more akin to the point you are now making.

So if you can, write the first chapter and the opening sentence without too much agonizing, knowing that you will come back to it. The aim is just to start and settle into the writing. I find that I can only start by writing myself into the mood, daft though it may sound. A fair amount of drivel arrives first, but I try to carry on without taking too much notice, trusting that I will reach a stage where I feel comfortable with my text. It does happen. Suddenly you are confident with your material and enjoying writing about episodes or characters. It is best not to stop and correct each page but just to keep going – in full flow. You can always go back and tidy text up later, but that delicious sense of being in control of the material and the writing may prove transitory if you fiddle with a typing mistake or check a spelling.

TRY THIS

■ Write up a section of prose you are just itching to have a go at!

■ Think up two different ways of opening the same biography.

16 | WORKING ON A CHAPTER

Planning each chapter

Not only would I advocate an outline plan for the whole book, I also think a plan for each chapter is vital. It probably goes without saying that you do need to have completed most of the research for the particular chapter you are going to write, before you write it. It doesn't matter that there are large research gaps further on in the life, but for this particular section you do need to feel confident that you are in possession of most of the salient facts. In practice, areas will probably crop up as you work that do require a bit more investigation – no problem.

What are you going to say?

Before I put pen to paper or switch on the computer, I ask myself a simple question. This is similar to the question that I ask when planning the book as a whole (see page 65). *What am I going to say in this chapter?* The question may appear simple, but often I cannot easily answer it. However, I firmly believe that I need to be able to answer the question in one sentence before I can start writing. I have learned the hard way (by spending days waffling around on paper that ultimately ends in the bin) that there is no point in writing a word until I have a concise answer.

Pinpointing your argument

What you are looking for in your answer is the *argument* or the *slant* that you are going to put on the material at your disposal. This is, after all, a biography and not a history. The aim of each chapter is to develop the previous one to build up a fully rounded, believable human being. Through your writing you are also seeking to help the reader understand the subject and arrive at the same conclusions that you have. You are not out to brain-wash or convert the reader, at least I don't think so. You are leading the reader through the same process of discovery and interpretation that you went through. Each chapter is a vital step in this journey.

I don't pretend that it is always easy to decide what the argument in each chapter is going to be. It can be terribly hard to look up from a particular document that you have been reading closely, and to let it recede back into the context of the whole life. Your chapter plan will tell you that a particular chapter is to cover, say, the five years your subject spent in France in her early twenties. Your research has told you what she did and who she met. From your chapter plan you also know roughly what is going into the following chapter. So, what you have to do is to create an overview of these five years – stand well away from the notes in your files – and try to decide how your subject developed.

I admit to wrestling for days, trying to see the situation clearly. I turn the details over in my head at all sorts of odd times. Washing up and walking the dogs can be particularly conducive to solving problems, whereas sitting at my desk and thinking about it doesn't seem to help me. It is fatal to re-read your notes, because it stirs up the pond again, when what you really needed is for everything to settle so that you can see the important features clearly.

When you can answer the question with a fairly straight-forward sentence, then you are off. Honestly the answer does come and I think you do know when you've cracked it. My experience has been (to use a cliché) that the light suddenly dawns. You *do* know what was going on during those five years in France, for example: she was trying to make a clean break with her family. So, now you have got all the facts in your head (and in your files) and they are going to flow out to create a picture.

Each chapter has to stand in its own right, as well as be an integral part of the life and the book. This is why it helps to look for an argument for *each* chapter and then select the material to support that argument. You are creating the outline plan for the chapter.

Don't put it in!

As has been mentioned before, the biggest temptation in biography writing is to put in everything you know just because you have painstakingly discovered it. The sad reality is that the majority of your research will never appear on the page. For instance, you may have the names of everyone at that fateful party in January 1746, know what they wore and ate, but don't include it. Your knowledge isn't wasted, though. It has enabled you to understand the sort of circles your subject moved in and to make an informed comment. So, you might say that he regularly socialized with members of the Catholic hierarchy who despised his ignorance. This is the sort of information your reader requires. You have chosen to include it, because you are developing a picture of a man who became strongly anti-clerical in later life and the reader needs to understand why this happened.

Don't ignore the inconvenient bits!

Whilst you may have developed an argument which seems to be working out well and you have selected material to support it, beware of ignoring the inconvenient bits. Sometimes your subject may do things which you cannot explain or which seem to contradict your interpretation. These things do have to be referred to and discussed. If you don't, a reviewer or an expert in the field will raise it and may undermine the whole credibility of your book. If you can't explain *why* your subject did something, say so. For example you could write: *It seems inexplicable that Johnson should have ... when he always thought that ...* Of course, if you have major misgivings about proceeding like this, perhaps the time has come to have another think about the central argument of your chapter. Could you have misread the evidence?

Let the subject speak

Do give your subject the chance to say a word or two, that is use their own words sometimes. You may be able to introduce a quotation from a letter or a diary at a certain point in the chapter. Not only does it bring the subject to life for the reader by letting them hear the subject's voice, but it also adds weight to your argument.

If possible, lift the quotation as direct speech with speech marks around it. For instance you might say *Jameson was getting very annoyed with the way the establishment received his work. 'If that's what they think of my Ceres painting,' he told his mistress, 'I'll not bother exhibiting at the Academy.'* By writing it in this way it appears that he was talking to her, when in reality you copied the quotation from a letter to her. This is legitimate and helps breathe life into the subject.

If, on the other hand, you cannot get permission to quote from the letter, you will have to paraphrase. No permission is needed in this case. So the same passage might now read, *Jameson was getting very annoyed with the way the establishment received his work. He told his mistress that he would not bother to exhibit at the Academy if that was what they thought of his Ceres painting.*

The extent to which you use quotations will, of course, depend on your intended reader. A children's biography will probably make limited use of quotations, whilst an academic biography might make extensive use. Quotations need to be integrated into the text carefully with attention to grammar. Check that the subject of your sentence and the subject in the quotation are compatible. The tenses or moods of verbs can also require you to manipulate your text so they fit in. It may be easier to use several short passages in preference to one long section. But, on occasions, there might be a good reason for quoting verbatim a large chunk of a letter or diary entry to allow the reader to appraise the situation first-hand. In this case, set the section of text apart as a paragraph on its own.

Don't be afraid to edit quotations to omit irrelevancies and to improve the flow. There are rules of punctuation which you should follow if you do this. Readers can then see where you have made changes. It would, of course, be immoral to edit out a section so that it distorted the meaning. Morality apart, it would discredit your book and your future writing if you did that.

Dates

You do need to keep the reader aware of the passage of time through the book. This is especially important in a biography which might use a whole chapter to discuss in depth the consequences of an afternoon and, in another chapter, cover the events of four years.

Putting the period of time that the chapter covers in brackets alongside its title or the chapter number is one helpful way. Another is just to periodically refer to the date. Instead of saying 'later in the May of that year she left for Nairobi' incorporate the year: 'Later in May 1912 she left for Nairobi'. Sometimes it is difficult to know how much to use dates as you write. Too many dates interrupt the flow of the narrative, like someone perpetually checking their watch. Look over your chapters when they are written and try to gauge where a date would be helpful.

National events

These also need to be included. They can be a subtle method of keeping the reader informed of the date: 'It was on the day of the opening ceremony of the Great Exhibition of 1851 that Gerald arrived in London'. This statement not only helps set the episode in time, but also enables the reader to link the episode to a known historical event, which assists your credibility. In this case, the reader might also sense the air of excitement in the capital as Gerald got off the train. You may also want to work in a national event that had no connection with your subject, but which would be well-known to the reader in order to give the narrative some sort of historical context. 'Whilst people in the capital worried about reports of the battles in the Crimea, in Surrey Gerald and his family were concerned about an outbreak of fowl pest that threatened to ruin their livelihood'.

Local events

Significant local events are also worth mentioning, not as dating aids but in order to give a flavour of the period. In my George Eliot research I remember coming across an account of discontent and rioting among the silk weavers in the Nuneaton area around the time she was born there. The account concerned a weaver being 'donkeyed' for accepting a low price for his goods. Further reading explained that the victim was tied onto a donkey facing its tail and paraded through the streets to the jeers and missiles of the crowd. Fights broke out and the yeomanry were called, then everyone melted away in terror. This account was brilliant for conveying the tensions of the time and I incorporated the extract in the chapter, even though the infant novelist probably never knew anything about it.

Be prepared

Because your research will be continuing throughout the writing, albeit on a lesser scale, be prepared to incorporate snippets of new material. It's strange how material turns up when you are not looking for it. You might be reading your subject's obituary, when you suddenly stumble across a useful reference to his school days. Maybe something he spoke of as an old man illuminates an incident from his early life. You might even discover there is a perfect little quotation you can weave in. If you don't want to stop writing the chapter you are currently working on in order to revise chapter two, make a note to go back to it. Attach a marker to the front sheet or insert the relevant notes in a plastic wallet in your file next to the chapter so you can sort it out at the end of the book's first draft.

Round it off

And finally, don't leave the reader high and dry at the end of a chapter. It is a temptation to stop when you have said what you want to say. A bit of tension or a cliff-hanger is fine, but remember that a chapter should stand in its own right. Look back to what you said when you opened the chapter to see if there are any threads you could draw together to round it off neatly. You are not looking for a grand finale, just a gentle conclusion to that period of the life or that episode.

TRY THIS

■ Think about one particular chapter you have planned and try to answer the question, 'What are you going to say in this chapter?'

---

17 | FINDING YOUR VOICE

What is your voice?

Your voice is basically your writing style. We all have one and it is as individual as our own spoken voice. But like your spoken voice it can vary. The way in which you speak to a policeman who has stopped you for speeding is different from the way you speak to an old school friend or to the postman. The same person is speaking in each case, but you vary your language, sentence construction and familiarity. We all adapt our speech to suit the situation and the audience. Writing is no different. So much of what was said in Chapter 12 about considering your reader comes into its own now.

It's not just about whether your reader is a child or an adult. It is also to do with the reason the reader has picked up your book in the first place. My voice for this particular book is different from the one I use in biography writing. I consider that the reader of this book has a *general interest* in the subject and has picked up the book to learn how to write biography more as a *hobby* than as an academic discipline. So I have aimed for an easy-going, chatty but informative style – you can judge whether I have got that right! That has meant that, from a purely technical point of view, I have written sentences that start with 'and' and 'but', thrown in asides and asked questions rhetorically or gone ahead and answered them myself. I have used a lot of sub-headings for ease of reference and avoided complex sentence constructions, long chapters and esoteric (whoops there's one) words. This is a conscious choice of style and a very easy one for me. I am addressing you as if you were sitting in front of me in a writer's workshop.

By contrast, if this had been one of my biographies I would have settled into a different voice. For instance, I would not have started a sentence with a conjunction, indeed I would have tried to be grammatically accurate in my writing. I would also have chosen more difficult words. That's not because I want to show off that I know them, but because biography is a form of literature and language is beautiful. Some words can be savoured and used to good effect. I get a real buzz out of writing a well-balanced sentence that contains some neat turns of phrase.

That sort of writing rarely appears on the page first-time round. The best use of language comes during textual revisions. So don't lose heart if what you have written appears mundane in the early stages. I tend to think the aim of a first draft is just to get it down on paper, often the hardest part. Strangely redrafting and polishing up are always easier than expected. I have to laugh inwardly writing this, because I still agonize over exactly what I am going to write every time I start, then think it is pretty rubbishy as it flows on to the paper. Yet, I tell myself not to panic: once there's something on paper to work with, the finished result is not too far away.

Get inside your subject

The voice you are looking for in biography writing is your own. Just be yourself. Do resist the temptation to think that your biography will have more gravitas if the style is pompous. It won't. It'll just put the reader off!

In your writing you are aiming to get inside your subject's head, or at least make the reader think that's where you are. The reader wants to know exactly what makes the subject tick. When you write about an event that happened to your subject, you should try to see it through their eyes, not from the outside. Easier said than done, I know, but I believe that this is a crucial difference between writing biography and writing history.

If, for instance, I were going to write about the time George Eliot (known as Marian Evans at the time) first met George Henry Lewes, I could state that they first met in a bookshop in 1852, which would be accurate but bland. I think a more exciting way of dealing with the meeting is to get behind the eyes of one of the characters and *imagine* what they saw in front of them. Yes, I did say imagine. This is where biography moves away from history and travels towards fiction.

To achieve the descriptions like the one below I look at photographs and portraits, and read collections of comments other people have made about the people concerned: their appearance, characteristics and behaviour. Then I create an *imaginary* meeting:

> *'She imagined him as a dashing Byronesque figure. Her romantic image was shattered when she encountered him in a bookshop in Piccadilly. The person Chapman introduced her to was an ugly little man who looked out from a tangle of beard, hair and moustache and resembled in her words more "a miniature Mirabeau" than any statuesque Byron. To her amusement, Chapman reported that the Carlyles had nicknamed Lewes the "Ape" because he always looked shaggy and could never sit still for five minutes. Marian found it hard to credit that this was the womanizer Bray had told her about. Lewes's wiry body lacked any obvious physical attractions and those parts of his face which showed through the curly mass of hair indicated a complexion ravaged by smallpox. She admitted he had expressive eyes; moreover his manner of addressing her conveyed the impression he had singled her out particularly for attention. Marian, wiser as a result of her experiences with Chapman, was not taken in. Over the following weeks she observed Lewes at various social gatherings turning exactly the same charm on all women he met. She dismissed him from her thoughts.'*

Of course I wasn't there. I don't know if that's what George Eliot thought at the time – it probably wasn't! But the value of such a description is that the reader now has a strong sense of Lewes's appearance, some knowledge of his character and feels that they have been taken into George Eliot's confidence by being made privy to her thoughts.

It is a fine line between *totally* making something up and using evidence gleaned from research to recreate a scene or a person's reaction. You just have to be as honest as you can.

Don't forget they are human!

It is easy to forget that the subject of your biography is, or was, a human being. This is especially important when their achievements have been outstanding and the world lauds them as a hero or heroine. Try to keep it in mind that you are writing about a real person who experienced the same emotions that other humans do. There must have been times when they were frightened, or jealous, or behaved in a way they later regretted.

There is a huge temptation to be very reverential towards great people: biographers in the past certainly were. But biography writing has changed since nineteenth-century hagiography. In those days biographies were written in order to inspire readers to emulate the idealized behaviour of the hero or heroine. Consequently any failings in their personality, even any humanity in them, were overlooked in favour of laudable virtues. Nobody wanted to know that Florence Nightingale was a bossy boots or that Lord Palmerston couldn't keep his hands off Queen Victoria's maids at Balmoral.

Today biographies should show all sides of the subject's personality. That means acknowledging their weaknesses and foibles as well as their virtues. Only then does the subject come alive for the reader. And revelations about the personality don't detract from the greatness of the achievement, which stands in its own right.

Get your subject down from the pedestal because up there they are cold and lifeless. What the reader wants is a human being. It is hard to be inspired by somebody who is unbelievably flawless. We want the truth, the living, breathing, sinful character, who does make mistakes, does have foibles, does find life difficult, but ultimately triumphs. Only that sort of person is believable in our world.

Humour

Light touches of humour make a text more readable and can offer you an alternative method of dealing with an event. But humour is a difficult thing to handle and what one person thinks is funny, another may not. Or worse, a third person may find offensive. So for that reason, proceed carefully.

You may find humour comes naturally from the irony of a situation. It might be that your subject is busy pursuing one course of action when, all the time, something else is taking place that they are unaware of. This is where the biographer, with the benefit of hindsight and a wide-angle lens, can make the most of a situation. I recall one character in a biography I was writing who was a pillar of the church, churchwarden, the lot. But at the same time he had a discreet business lending money (and charging interest) to impecunious clergymen. I found that funny and so added the line: 'He thought it was part of his Christian duty to help those in need in the parish.' Some people might have thought I was cruel, but I had a feeling that I was making the sort of observation that someone at the time might have made to a neighbour or friend.

So do use humour if it comes naturally. But don't go looking for jokes to include! If humour is used gently, it might serve to sharpen up an observation you want to make. Most of all resist the temptation to send people up.

Can you criticize your subject?

Returning to the image of the subject up there on the pedestal, I think you can sling some mud around. I'd say mud, rather than stones, because if your criticism is too strong, you may end up destroying the subject completely. Whilst it is your job to acknowledge the subject's weaknesses and failings, there must have been a large part of their personality and achievements that you admired to make you want to write the book. So that has to come through and outweigh all the failings – or you may have written yourself out of a book.

When you are criticizing your subject for their thoughts or actions, it is vital that you also get inside their head. Try to let the reader understand *why* the subject behaved as they did, misguided though it was. It is vital your reader remains sympathetic to the subject and is prepared to understand and forgive. Otherwise they may not finish the book, or buy your next one!

Be fair

The overriding concern, I think, is to be honest and fair to your subject. They can't answer back or explain their actions, so it's down to you to put their case, however wrong it seemed.

As well as being fair to your subject, you must be fair to your reader. By reading your text in the first place, the reader has placed their trust in you to check the facts and make judgements on their behalf. If you abuse that trust you do so at your own peril.

TRY THIS

■ Use a picture of an event to write a paragraph of around 250 words about what was going on as one of the people in the picture might have glimpsed it.

■ Work over that paragraph to strengthen the power of the description by changing a few words.

---

18 | AUTOBIOGRAPHY

An enjoyable hobby

Autobiography is a very popular art form especially amongst retired people who have enjoyed a varied life and want to record it for posterity. I have met many people in writers' groups involved in this sort of writing: there are always more autobiographers than biographers. But that's fine. It's an enjoyable hobby and an excellent way of passing information on in the family.

Only in rare cases are autobiographies published. That certainly doesn't matter. Publication is not the be all and end all of writing. Many people write because they enjoy the discipline and get pleasure from reading their work back to others in a group. That is how autobiography is best regarded. Very few publishers accept the autobiography of an unknown person, no matter how exciting their life. There have been a few autobiographies of ordinary people with exceptional connections or a truly extraordinary tale to tell. I find it much kinder to advise the would-be autobiographer to write for the pleasure of it. If they do succeed in getting their work published then that's a bonus.

Research

This might seem an odd heading to put down in this chapter. After all, the author knows all about themselves better than anybody. Nevertheless, it's probably worth making a timeline (see page 19). Write down the key events in your life and alongside note significant things which were happening to other members of your family, as well as local and national events you might want to mention. This will help to anchor the narrative at various points.

As you work you may be surprised to discover that you do need to do additional research. You may have taken things for granted when you were a child and now need to check them out. Was Aunty Glad actually a relative? How old was the elderly lady next door? And what actually was it that 'we don't talk about'? Ages of relatives and specific information about the school you attended might be required. There are probably family and friends you could ask for snippets of information, or to give their version of events. Like witnesses to a crime, it is amazing how many different accounts of what *actually* happened there are. That can be quite disconcerting, but in this instance what really matters is *your* version of the event, it is after all your story.

Picture research

This is likely to be easier than it might be for a biographer because you probably have access to lots of unofficial family archives. The families of friends from the past are also worth contacting. It is wonderful how many different photographs of scenes and people can be unearthed this way. Don't be afraid to ask around. People usually love digging out pictures but be prepared to spend ages on your visits. Pictures can set you off on a new course of enquiry or jog a memory that you had completely forgotten about. The niggling thing is that all too often pictures don't have any information written on the back. You get that superb photograph of a group of three friends but the name of the centre person, the one they have all got their arms linked with, is a total mystery. Infuriating!

I think with autobiography old photographs make the story come alive. References to Aunty Beatty's antics with the village grave digger are all the more engrossing when we can look at the matronly lady, all togged up in her Sunday best, posing for the camera. It's not just photographs of people that are helpful. The houses where people lived, early views of the village street or a line of long-gone shops, all play their part in recreating the scenes of childhood alongside your description.

Maps can be a particularly useful adjunct. I would be very tempted to draw my own, based on an existing large scale map perhaps, but one which included my personal landmarks so it fitted in with the narrative. My map would show the tree I fell out of when I was six and the brook behind the boggy bit of land we called 'Gassy Moors', where the purple orchids flowered. All this is wonderfully evocative.

Planning

In many ways planning is even more important than research because it may be that you choose only to write about a particular period in your life: that time when you were with the jungle patrol in Malaya or your childhood spent travelling the world with hippy parents for example. The research and construction have to be tailored to fit.

Some autobiographers find that planning takes the fun out of it. The writing is a journey of discovery and, until they have written it, they are not sure what they can remember. That's absolutely fine. It's your story and, like all the tips in this book, they are just suggestions. What is most important is to discover the way that works best for you and go along with it. The danger, or the fun, of autobiography is that you discover there is loads more you can say about an incident, or a period of your life, than you originally thought. Without any planning the proposed book can become unwieldy or shapeless. If the book is intended for sharing with others (or even for publication) then planning and structure must be a major feature of the early stages. If the autobiography is for fun and posterity then write it and enjoy it!

Try the easy approach

Many autobiographers in writers' groups have begun to write their life story by accident. Perhaps sparked off by a task set by the tutor and believing they couldn't come up with a good idea themselves, they have adapted something that happened to them, which is the way many good novelists work. Then, when the 'short story' has been read back to the group, it has been received with such interest that the author is inspired to carry on.

Just writing one small incident from your childhood as a story is a great way to start. You do not have to think about whether you can write a whole book or precisely how long your piece should be. The story can be complete in itself and will dictate its own length and style. That's freedom.

If you wish you can go on to write other stories from your past taking any incident and dramatizing it. Remember the smells, the colours and the taste of things. They always seem to have been so much more vivid when you were a child. Try and work in something of these sensations where you can.

Each story can be complete in its own right and you need make no attempt to link them together. They can be like snapshots in an old photograph album, small but full of tantalizing details. Or, once written, you can rework them so they flow from one to the other. The danger with autobiographical writing is that it is addictive. I've not met anyone who has written one autobiographical story then got bored. What often happens is that it opens the floodgates to loads more stories or that the writer decides to move into fiction taking their experiences and manipulating them to serve a different purpose.

Finding your voice

With autobiography it is traditional to write in the first person but not everyone feels comfortable doing this. Some people find it easier to write in the third person: 'He set out for Australia at the age of thirteen …'. Thing are related in the way you might write fiction. This has the advantage of being able to change names and slightly alter pieces that could be sensitive. Somehow it seems less dishonest to do this in the third person than it does in the first person. But of course there's no compulsion to be absolutely honest in autobiography. It's your life and you can say whatever you like, indeed the reader brings a different expectation to autobiography for that reason. In the writing of biography you do have an obligation to be truthful and honest.

One of the main difficulties about writing autobiography is that the people who are mentioned in it may well be around to read what you say about them. Fine if those comments are complimentary, but a possible problem if you have chosen to state a few home truths. But it's worth remembering that you can write your autobiography without circulating it right away.

Writing it up

You can be flexible when writing up an autobiography that's not for publication. Whilst you can use the same style as a biography, you could consider producing something more along the lines of an illustrated coffee table book. A coffee table book is only a glossy scrapbook with lots of illustrations: photographs, maps and other memorabilia like programmes, souvenirs and postcards. The text is used to elaborate on the pictures. Some writers and many readers of the unpublished autobiography may find this an appealing way of presenting the life-story. It's your life, your choice!

TRY THIS

■ Take an incident from your school days that sticks in your mind and write up a short story.

■ Use one of your old holiday photographs and write a short story about an incident on that holiday.

19 | SEX

Do you have sex?

This might seem a very personal question but it is the concern of today's biographer. You may not have set out to write an erotic biography but sex is a normal part of life and if you are writing a life story, surely it has a part.

Once again this is an area where styles of writing biography have changed dramatically over the years. No Victorian biography would have mentioned this topic, no matter how much influence it had on the life and work of the subject. Georgie Burne-Jones, who wrote *Memorials of Burne-Jones* as a two-volumed biography of her husband, was extremely careful to omit all reference to the affair he had with the model Marie Zambaco. He actually ran off as far as Dover with the Greek woman, only to be fetched back by William Morris. Obviously Georgie was writing for the market at the time and anything else would have been unprintable. She also wanted to preserve her husband's reputation and, to some extent, her own. But, just as she was writing for the contemporary market so must we.

When Freud suggested that high achievement might be linked with sexual repression, that was exactly the invitation biographers had been waiting for. Suddenly the whole area of the subject's private life was private no more, but essential for understanding the subject. And it was an acceptable topic for public discussion. Woe betide any biographer now who fails to consider this aspect of their subject's life.

How much sex do you have?

There is no correct answer. Advertisers know that most people are interested in sex; their own and other people's. Consequently, sex is used to sell anything from a joint of meat to a car and, apparently, it succeeds. Of course sex does sell books, from the revelations about a politician's sexual proclivities to the erotic novel. Obviously dragging loads of sexual detail into a biography just to boost sales would not be in the best tradition of biography writing – but who said you have to follow tradition? It's your biography, your choice.

The decision about how much sexual detail to include in your biography will depend on the extent to which sex dominated your subject's life and influenced their activities. In the case of a musician who spent all his spare time in bars and clubs pursuing women, then this was a major preoccupation. Consequently it would loom large in the biography, possibly with some explicit information about what he actually did when he caught his quarry. Linked into that, the reader would expect to find some consideration of how these sexual exploits influenced the subject's musical output.

Graphic details? Yes, if necessary. Whilst maybe you did not set out to titillate the reader with explicit detail, they may feel short-changed if you lead them to the bedroom, slam the door, give them plenty of creaking and shrieking, but fail to explain what was actually going on.

You need to consider the reader you had in mind. Obviously, with a child reader sexual detail has to be very circumspect. Whilst you should not tell lies, sex is probably an area you should not stray into at all. In the academic or literary biography, you would need to judge the relevance of sexual detail to the area you decided to focus on. But the biography written for the 'average reader' predominantly to entertain may, in your judgement, require more sexual detail.

There is always the issue of how comfortable you feel writing about someone else's sex life. If you are not easy with it, perhaps there are some primary sources you could quote from that would enable the reader to interpret the evidence themselves. It is a great help to read established biographers and be guided by the way they have handled sensitive topics.

Assistance may be on the way!

Advances in DNA testing, which is now widely used in crime detection, are having a surprising impact on the world of biography.

It is still early days yet. But over a decade ago historians were aware of the possibilities of extracting genetic material from Egyptian mummies for analysis. More recently Martin Bormann's son gave blood samples to prove that a skull discovered by builders near the Führerbunker was indeed that of his father. The result? Many biographies with details of Bormann's supposed life in South America were instantly discredited. It was also DNA evidence that ended Anna Anderson's claim to be Anastasia, the last remaining member of the Russian royal family. That killed off the biographies about her.

You might be wondering where sex comes into all this. Posthumous revelations about the sex life of American President Thomas Jefferson have recently come to light as a result of tests on DNA samples given by his descendants. These confirmed the truth of a rumour that he had indeed fathered a child on one of his black servants.

Even when there are no descendants, evidence can still be gleaned from unexpected sources. It seems the purchase of a lock of Beethoven's hair at Sotheby's enabled a scientist to claim the great musician died of syphilis, a condition which can lead to deafness. Analysis of 19 hairs trapped in Shakespeare's alleged death mask has led one biographer to conclude the playwright died of cancer of the eye. What other revelations might be possible once a person's DNA has been isolated? Certainly, the idea that your subject took their guilty secrets to the grave is no longer a foregone conclusion.

TRY THIS

The mind runs riot at what tasks might be attempted in this chapter but ...

■ Look at the work of several established biographers to see how they have written about, or ignored, their subject's sexuality.

■ Do you think their writing was effective?

20 | BRIDGING THE GAP

An incomplete picture

No matter how carefully you do your research, there will be bits you can't uncover. It's a horrible thing to have to admit to yourself that you simply don't know what was going on. But it does happen. Now that doesn't mean you can't write your biography – unless of course the gaps cover most of the life! But what it does mean is that you are going to have to think of ways of bridging these gaps.

Don't make it up!

One thing you certainly *can't* do is to make up what happened. Whilst biography does employ some of the techniques of fiction, making up the plot isn't one of them!

You may well find it easier to be honest with your reader and say something like, 'Details of the time he spent in Athens are sketchy' or, 'Little is recorded about her relationship with the prince'.

Speculate

You are now free to lead on with your speculation about what *might* have happened, perhaps by continuing 'however it seems likely that ...'. In this way you are not misleading your reader, but you are giving them the benefit of your knowledge and research to make an informed guess about the situation. This is one of the reasons why it is important that you work on building up the reader's trust in your integrity and judgement as the biography progresses. Previous comments and information that you have given in the narrative have been supported by references to letters and other sources, so the reader has confidence in you.

When you are short of specific information on an area of the life, you are going to have to lean heavily on background research, as well as give a feeling of verisimilitude (one of my nice esoteric words meaning a feeling of real life). So to return to my subject who spent some time in Athens in 1810 doing I don't know what, I will begin with some reading about the city today just to get myself started. From that I will move back to the beginning of the nineteenth century to see if it was significantly different then. What would be the key features of the city that might have caught my subject's eye? What could I comment on? Now, I can't say he visited the Acropolis, because I don't know. But knowing my subject adored everything classical I could say, 'He visited Athens, whose great antiquities would have appealed to one so steeped in history. The Acropolis was …'. Then I would add a brief description of it using present-day photographs, old etchings and possibly an early nineteenth-century written account of the Parthenon.

Further research might supply me with information about other significant people living in the city or visiting it around that time. That would also help to set this specific event into context, even though I have no knowledge of whether my subject actually met them or even knew of their existence.

Moving from the zoom lens to the wide-angle lens, you would look back at your timeline to see whether there were any events international, national, local or personal that you could refer to. Local in this case would be local to Athens. For instance did my subject's visit coincide with a smallpox epidemic or a severe drought? Perhaps there was some civil disruption I could make mention.

Then, moving back further, was there an international happening I ought to include? As my subject was notionally staring up at the caryatids, was Wellington leading his army against Napoleon, or was the country smarting from some defeat the previous year?

If nothing of note was happening on the international front, were there any events my reader could relate to in Britain? If my subject is entwined in the arms of her Spanish prince, could the British government, unbeknown to her, be concerned that revolution might be spreading to England?

Now, I know you could argue that dragging in events like this is irrelevant, simply filling up paper for the sake of it. That could be true if you are not careful. But set against that you are faced with a blank period in your subject's life and you have a book to write. Just stating 'I don't know what happened here' is not very satisfying for the reader. Having immersed them well and truly in the life, persuaded them to accept you as the expert, the safe pair of hands, you suddenly bring them up short with a jolt. You risk destroying your credibility as the biographer.

So I would suggest you try to glide your way over this gap with background research and some gentle speculation as to what might have caught your subject's eye or interest at this period.

Without being misleading, try to avoid too many 'he might have' or 'she probably went to …'. It is rather off-putting to read an excessive number of maybes.

Returning to the fictional subject who had an affair with the prince, you could resort to working from a picture of him to describe his appearance, augmented by other people's accounts of his clothing, stance and general bearing. You could also make use of the descriptions and pictures of the palace or the house where the affair took place. If you were really scratching around you might turn to material about some of the prince's close associates at the time leaving the general impression that the subject encountered them – but I would avoid stating that as a fact. The aim is to create the general atmosphere even though you have no actual hard evidence.

I'd be the first to admit that this is not the perfect way to write biography, but this chapter is about what to do when life is not perfect!

TRY THIS

■ Could you write half a page on the time your subject spent visiting London during the Second World War without any factual evidence of his activities?

■ Briefly describe a meeting between your subject and Henry VIII on the River Thames.

21 | CAN YOU SAY ANYTHING YOU LIKE?

Briefly: yes if your subject is dead and no if he or she is alive.

The Dead

Basically, once a person has died anyone can write or say what they like about them. The deceased are not covered by the laws of libel or slander. That does not mean that you go straight into a vitriolic diatribe against them in your biography. But it does allow you the freedom to make judgements about their behaviour or character that they might have challenged – with the full force of the law – had they been alive.

The Living

They are protected by the law, so it behoves you to take enormous care what you say. Anything which is considered to be a *defamatory statement* about an *identifiable living person* is *libel*. The court would be asked to consider whether what you said, overtly or by innuendo, exposed that person to hatred, ridicule or contempt. If you are concerned that something you have written may be challenged on these grounds, consider having it read for libel. This costs money but not as much as court action.

Responsibility

A word of warning on the subject of libel: don't presume it is the publisher's responsibility to check for libel. It probably isn't. Many publishers' contracts have a clause that place such matters (and their legal costs!) well and truly at your door. There are however various forms of libel insurance that can be purchased.

The friends and relatives

What has been said so far covers only the subject of your biography and may explain why I have always preferred my subjects well and truly dead! But as well as the subject, everyone mentioned in the book also has rights and these should be borne in mind. Modern-day descendants of your subject may take exception to what you say about them, their legitimacy or any other remarks which could be construed as defamatory. They have rights and could challenge your writings in court, so take care.

Skeletons in the cupboard

Skeletons in the cupboard can rattle around and cause you some anxiety. Not because you are scared of spooks, but because you are concerned about the living. If you come across some material that is incontestably true, should you write about it? This is always a difficult question to answer and one which other biographers have agonized over in the past. Some argue, in the cause of truth, what has been discovered should be published no matter what the relatives think. Truth will out!

Others urge caution on the grounds that this is only a book, written possibly to entertain or inform, and it is does not justify destroying someone's life by revealing information they would prefer hidden.

No easy answer

Suppose you are researching a new biography of a well-known playwright who died 20 years ago. In the course of your research you visit the widow who is most hospitable and helpful. She gives you free access to everything in her possession, including a suitcase of letters and papers that she has never looked at. You read through them and discover the playwright had an affair with his wife's sister, who appears to have been his muse for more than a decade. You suspect that the widow had no knowledge of this. What do you do?

If you publish this information the wife will feel publicly humiliated and her memory of her husband be permanently tarnished. Is that fair? Is destroying the living for the sake of a book acceptable?

The alternative is to ignore that information and publish a biography that is incomplete and misleading. Not only have you done your readers a disservice by suppressing information, you have failed to explain the playwright's inspiration for some major works. A biographer following you might publish those facts about the affair and discredit your book completely.

There is no easy answer. I am a coward and I always hope that I will never find myself in such a position. The respected biographer, Nigel Nicolson, who raised a similar hypothetical case, said he felt the feelings of the living should be taken into consideration. He would not publish information that was hurtful to the widow, but to cover himself against future criticism he would initial and date the relevant letters, then put them back in the suitcase.

How far do you consider family feelings?

Nicolson was clear that he would respect the feelings of the subject's contemporary relatives and the children, but not those of the grandchildren. What was published about their grandparents, he felt, would not do any great harm to them.

A few years ago the biographer, Fiona McCarthy, faced a similar situation with her biography of the art–craftsman, Eric Gill. Her research revealed a voracious sexual appetite for various women and even the family dog, but worst of all the sexual abuse of his daughters. Gill had been dead for some time when her biography was published, nevertheless there was a tremendous outcry when McCarthy revealed these details about the pious Roman Catholic craftsman. Even greater condemnation followed when it emerged some of the daughters were still alive. However, these ladies had actually given their permission for the information to be made public.

TRY THIS
- What would you have done if faced with the suitcase of letters?

22 | SELECTING PICTURES AND WRITING CAPTIONS

Picture research

Publishers are obviously the people who have the final say on which pictures are to be used for publication, but they still need your recommendations. If the book is not destined for publication, then you have a totally free hand. Either way, you need to be thinking about possible pictures and collecting details all through your research and writing. As discussed previously, you will need pictures for your information as you write, not just to use as final illustrations.

Points to remember

Pictures cost money to reproduce, more money than text does. Equally, colour pictures cost more to reproduce than black and white, but on the plus side costs are coming down with each technological advance. If the biography, autobiography or family history is to be published by you, at your expense, then this is a very significant consideration. For very small print runs, such as an autobiography or family history designed for family circulation, you might choose to order duplicate prints of original photographs, make colour photocopies or even scan them into a computer to print.

What is the correct number of pictures?

This is similar to the question 'how long is a piece of string?', but there are some guidelines. Apart from costs already mentioned, one very important consideration is the nature of the biography. What type of book did you set out to write? Obviously the coffee-table type is dependent on a large number of high quality pictures – the quality of the illustrations is the major selling feature. The text serves the illustrations.

At the other end of the spectrum might be a political biography where the text is of paramount importance. It would make no difference to the success of such a book if there were no pictures at all. In between there are biographies of all sorts of people, some of whom led very visual lives. The biography of the sculptor or the film star requires illustrations of their work or of them in different roles to augment the text.

Biographies designed for children probably need a reasonable number of pictures, whereas the same subject for an adult could use less. Let's face it, most of us enjoy studying pictures. There is also that old adage *a picture is worth a thousand words*. It does hold some truth, but I would not agree with it totally or we are all out of a job! When someone picks up a book in a shop deciding whether or not to buy, the visual impact looms large. The cover will probably catch their attention first. Then they'll flick through looking at odd pictures. Only then, if they are still interested, will they read the blurb on the jacket to decide whether they want it. As writers, we may might think these are not good reasons for choosing a book, but that's often how it happens, so the number and choice of pictures is important.

Blocks or singles?

Ideally the pictures should be spread through the book, coming near to the text they illuminate. However, that is in the best of all possible worlds, or in your own publication where you have total control. When a publisher is involved, he or she has the ultimate say on picture numbers and distribution. Because of the way printing technology works, pictures may have to be placed in a block together. The way picture pages are printed, folded and cut usually dictates that the picture section comes in blocks of four pages (that is eight sides). You may be lucky enough to persuade a publisher to let you have two such blocks set apart in the text, one to cover the early life and one the later.

What sort of pictures do you choose?

Pictures of the subject at different stages of their life are going to be useful. How easy these are to get will depend on the historical period and, possibly, the affluence of the family involved. Pictures of your Jacobean subject as a baby may be a tall order, but faintly possible if father was the Earl of Somewhere and commissioned a family portrait complete with wife and swaddled baby.

Victorian baby photographs are not that common either. Whether it was because infant mortality was high or that exposures were so long you couldn't keep a baby still, I am not sure. Once you are into the twentieth century you stand a better chance of having your wish granted. However, having a photograph taken of yet another mouth to feed would have been out of reach for the working-class father in the 1930s.

With some subjects photographs can be scarce. When I was researching Edith Holden, the Country Diary lady, I gratefully published anything and everything that turned up with the lady herself in it. There was no thoughtful selection of baby, teenage, marriage or middle-aged portrait for me. If your subject is the Queen then you have the opposite problem. The requirement is to find a picture no one has seen before, or one where the facial expression conveys a lot of meaning.

It is infuriating when you do find a photograph of the subject but they are standing amongst a group of unknown people. It also tests your ingenuity to the limit to write a meaningful caption that doesn't simply highlight your ignorance! If nothing else, the exercise does teach you the value of writing on the back of your own family photographs for the sake of posterity – and yes, your future biographer!

Other portraits

In addition to pictures of the subject themselves, it can be interesting to show their parents and siblings. I would not advise lots of pictures of them, unless there is a good reason. The same goes for other relatives, indeed I wouldn't choose to include the aunt, the uncle, the cousins and so on, unless they were especially relevant. Choose a photograph that includes the relative with the subject, if at all possible.

We automatically think of photographs of modern subjects, but do not forget there could be paintings or sculptures. A cartoon or caricature can also be very effective because, by its very nature, it is designed to say something about the personality.

Significant friends, especially if they are well-known figures in their own right, are worth including. Ideally, depict them at the age and as they were when your subject encountered them. Think of the would-be purchaser flicking through a copy of your biography in the bookshop. If they see a portrait of Tennyson or Marilyn Monroe amongst the illustrations, that might well clinch the sale. But the illustration really does have to be relevant!

Location shots

A series of illustrations that contain nothing but people can get rather tedious, so vary them. The house where your subject lived is of interest to the reader and gives variety to your picture selection. How it looked at the time is best, but may not be possible. A modern-day photograph will work provided you caption as such: the satellite dish and Ferrari on the drive of Dickens's former residence may confuse the reader.

It can be infuriating to locate a property after much documentary research and foot slogging, only to discover it was demolished in the 1960s. All may not be lost. Local studies libraries may have a photograph of it, so too might the National Monuments Record Centre mentioned in Chapter 8.

When selecting any possible illustrations bear in mind they are likely to be reproduced in black and white and possibly reduced in size to a quarter page. Consider whether they will still have something to offer the reader. Extraneous material at the sides can be trimmed off. Pictures of buildings usually work fairly well, but the same may not be true of landscapes reduced in size and reproduced in black and white.

Before we leave the topic of locations think about the sort of activity your subject was involved in. A photograph of a typical nineteenth-century operating theatre, albeit one of a museum display and definitely not one your subject ever went near, could nevertheless help the reader visualize the scene. Another source of illustration for a typical operating theatre might be a nineteenth-century painting or a line drawing from a contemporary periodical.

Picture agencies

Many exist and can provide transparencies for reproduction of almost any subject you could name – at a price. The price varies with the scarcity of the subject; whether the picture has been reproduced before or is guaranteed to be unpublished; whether it is for a book or for merchandise; whether the rights are for one country alone or world-wide. It is a bit of a minefield. In practice, getting pictures from an agency isn't your problem. If they are required, the publisher sorts out the mechanics of loaning them. However, the publisher might want you to make suggestions about the pictures that they borrow from the agencies.

Collect as you go

This topic has been mentioned before as part of the research (see page 41). It doesn't matter in the slightest that your copy of the picture is just a photocopy or a postcard you bought at a stately home. All you need is something to show an editor so that they can see what is available and whether it might be suitable. If the opportunity presents itself, purchase a transparency if you think it might be useful. These are sometimes for sale in museums, art galleries and other tourist attractions for a nominal sum. Whilst you most certainly *cannot* reproduce it without permission, it is often relatively easy to get permission and you have a high quality picture without any of the complications of arranging a professional shoot.

Captions

These are more important than people think. Have you read a caption that, frankly, doesn't tell you anything? 'Queen Mary with her dog' is perfectly obvious to anyone looking at the picture. 'Queen Mary aged six with her dog' is unlikely to excite the reader or any would-be purchaser flicking through the book. An improvement might be 'Queen Mary posing with Scruffy, whom she had rescued from a dung heap as a puppy.'

Captions should add information, entertain and, if possible, intrigue the reader. One I had fun with was for a picture of Stanley

Baldwin as a little boy. I came across a photograph of him in a short skirt with blonde curls like a girl, standing on a chair. On closer inspection I could see he was holding a biscuit in his hand. So the caption read 'England's future Prime Minister, Stanley Baldwin, bribed by a biscuit to pose for the camera. He was aged three and taken out of skirts the following year.' It was a great picture and caught the eye of several reviewers, one of whom headed his review 'Stanley Takes the Biscuit' even though the book was actually about Baldwin's mother and her sisters.

Captions can be difficult to write, especially when you are faced with 50 to produce over a weekend. It may help to look through other biographies and see what was written and how you reacted to them. That can give you ideas about what to emulate and what to avoid.

Using extracts from quotations can be helpful with portraits and prevent you being forced to state the obvious. This solved my problem with one typically stern looking Victorian portrait: 'Edward Poynter, "whom some perhaps might not call a pleasant man, when he talks to himself always says yes most amiably, and that's about the only time he ever does say it," declared his brother-in-law, Burne-Jones and most people agreed with him.'

Do you have to write in sentences?

It isn't vital to use full sentences in a caption. 'Jane's house in 1834' is perfectly acceptable. If you are aiming for a slightly more informative caption, then a couple of sentences might well be preferable, but two sentences are probably the limit. The picture is the main attraction and is being reproduced on expensive glossy paper, so you have got to resist the temptation to write a short essay. It's a balancing act but one that is well worth attempting to get right.

TRY THIS
- Select several pictures and write captions.
- To test your abilities further choose all landscapes to caption!

The title

The title is enormously important. I won't claim it's the bit that sells the book, but a snappy title does add to the book's appeal. I think it's rather like your name being you, and if you were called something else, you would feel like a different person. Well, rather whimsically I tend to feel the same about my books. Admittedly it's always after the event because during their research and writing they are generally anonymous – like the child in the womb who is only named once it is born.

Who names the book?

Not you, I'm sorry to say. The title often comes from the marketing department at the publishers. Apparently sales people, who probably haven't read the book, have the best ideas about titles that sell. But having said that your ideas are generally listened to and noted.

You have probably pondered on the title at odd times during your research. The book may have started out as *A Biography of Tennyson*, or whoever, but then you start to toy with possible titles. It can indeed remain as *Alfred Lord Tennyson: a biography*. Many successful biographies have carried the name of the person as the title and nothing else. Others have begun with a phrase and had the subject's name as the subtitle, hence *The Edwardian Lady – the story of Edith Holden*.

This title of my first book was not my invention. In fact, whilst I was researching and writing, the book was untitled. I never believed it would ever be published, so I did not concern myself with a title! When it did get to the stage of needing a title, I did my best to come up with something. I knew that nobody had ever heard of Edith Holden, but everybody knew the best-selling *The Country Diary of an Edwardian Lady*, so clearly that had to be incorporated in the title. I still couldn't work it out. Everything seemed long and cumbersome.

What actually happened was that Webb & Bower, the publishers, suggested the title based on something the American publisher of *Country Diary* used to say when he passed through their office to check on the progress of that book. His opening remarks were frequently, 'Hi folks, how's the Edwardian lady doing?' So the name was carried over to her biography. At the time I thought it was rather flat but now, having lived with it for 20 years, like my own name, I can't imagine it called anything else. It is the book.

As a researcher though, I know it's a pain trying to locate a biography that doesn't carry the subject's name prominently in the title and that has influenced my own approach to biography titles ever since. I now prefer to have the subject's name first, so the book will get filed in the biography section of the library and bookshop under the surname of the subject: where people expect to find it and where the subject name will show up clearly on the spine. However, I do like a sub-title that's got some element of intrigue to whet the reader's appetite. Such a sub-title will also help to distinguish this biography of Charles II from the other six published this century.

In some instances a book can bear a completely different title in the US from the UK edition, depending what each marketing department thinks is right for their market.

Don't worry if you never arrive at a suitable title yourself. Give the manuscript a working title to send it off with so the poor child has some identity, but ultimately the title will be outside your control anyway.

Occasionally you get a flash of inspiration. The one I'm most pleased with is a text book I wrote on rites of passage. I literally woke up one morning and thought *The Time of Your Life!*, that would be great. And luckily the editor agreed. Well-known expressions can prove a fruitful source of inspiration for titles. You can just take snippets from them, leaving the reader to recognize and complete the well-known phrase or saying.

Another point worth making is that titles are not protected by copyright, so you may choose a title that has already been used. There are, however, some situations where a title cannot be used for another book. This applies where the title has distinctive wording like *Swallows and Amazons*, rather than a purely descriptive title like *The Life of King Harold*. So, a person buying *Swallows and Amazons* is likely to be under the impression they are getting the one written by Arthur Ransome. For further advice on this The UK Society of Authors produces a useful quick guide to *The Protection of Titles* which can be purchased by non-members.

Chapter names

Chapters don't have to have names at all. It is a matter of personal preference. Some authors just number their chapters, others give the chapter a name, even a synopsis of the contents and, in the case of biography, dates. I think the fashion for a synopsis of the contents has gone but there could be a case for it in an academic work. When considering your reader, you may feel the biography is going to be used as much for reference as read straight through. A chapter synopsis would save the student time as they scan the contents of the chapter to check whether it fulfils their requirements.

My own preference is to put the dates that the chapter covers in brackets after each chapter title. I feel it gives the reader a point of reference. It is also useful to the student trying to locate information quickly.

How you choose the title for a chapter is again down to personal preference. As you are researching you can note useful little phrases that have occurred in letters, which might make a clever title. At one stage in my *Victorian Sisters* biography as I was working on the growing relationship between two of the characters, I kept coming across the Pre-Raphaelite obsession with the Arthurian legend and the mediaeval concept of courtly love. Courtly love seemed a good phrase for a chapter heading and by adding a question mark to it, I could make the reader consider the difference between what the Pre-Raphaelites preached and what they practised.

At one stage in George Eliot's life she was very interested in the early feminist movement which, in the mid-nineteenth century, was referred to as *The Woman Question*. It seemed ironic that, as George Eliot was busy discussing the Woman Question, she was actually even more busily hunting for a man. So I titled that particular period of her life *The Man Question* hoping my readers could enjoy the joke with me.

It can be helpful if the chapter has a name when you are following up a reference at the back of a book. I find it much easier to remember a name than whether I am looking for Chapter 10 or Chapter 11.

TRY THIS

■ Enjoy yourself composing titles for biographies.

■ Are there any clever titles you can create from a well-known saying that would be appropriate for a particular subject?

24 | WRITING FOR CHILDREN

A distinct market

People tend to assume that writing means books for adults, but don't automatically dismiss the children's market for biography. It certainly does exist and children's books can often make a bigger impact on their readers, and are better remembered than many things we read as adults. Indeed, you can probably remember books about famous people that you read when you were younger far better than you can adult biographies. Not only do some children read biographies for pleasure, but the books are also much in demand for school project work and, as such, are bought by schools and public libraries. So you could be looking at a reasonably wide market and a longer shelf life than a similar book written for an adult audience.

Just because a biography is aimed at the child reader doesn't in any way alter its validity. In no sense is this the market for a writer who has failed in the adult arena – writing for the child reader is a skilled art-form.

Choosing a subject

In many ways the method of choosing a subject is similar to that already discussed in Part One. The age of the child reader may well determine their interests and so might their gender, though I hesitate at making such a politically incorrect statement! In the past there certainly were strong stereotypical assumptions that boys liked one sort of subject and girls another, which did both a disservice. Today children's books should be written with both sexes in mind, but I think it is worth being aware that some subjects will naturally appeal more to girls than to boys, or vice versa.

When thinking about a subject for a children's biography it might be worthwhile looking to see what historical figures are included in school work at various levels. This would certainly assist sales.

People who have achieved amazing feats of endurance always fascinate and inspire children, although it is no longer appropriate to use biographies for children as a back door way of setting a moral example.

Popular heroes amongst children tend to come from the world of sport and entertainment, so if you have a particular interest and, hence, knowledge in one of those areas, it might be worth developing this. The biography that comes out at the right time can do extremely well, but beware that such interests are fashionable and ephemeral; the timing has to be exactly right. A book about a sporting hero that comes out three months after he has been dropped by the team may suffer a similar fate with potential readers.

Language

One significant way in which a biography written for children is going to be different will be in the level of language used. Talking to children in the age group you are writing for will help you gain an awareness of their linguistic ability, as does reading books designed for this age group. Writing for your own children, grandchildren or some you know well will also ensure you get the right feel. Children require to be told the truth and should not be patronized in the telling.

Dialogue

When writing for children, you are likely to use shorter sentences and a simpler sentence construction than in a corresponding adult biography. Another significant difference will be the use of dialogue. It often works well in children's writing to use dialogue to convey some of the information directly.

In an adult biography you might well jib at putting words into the mouth of your subject, or indeed in anyone's mouth, unless you had strong evidence that this was what was actually said on that occasion. Even then, if you had good reason to believe a person said such a thing, you might still opt for reported speech: 'Thomas Telford said he could no longer work with these design restrictions.' If this book was for children of school age you would need to be more direct: '"I can't do this work if I'm not allowed to have a free hand," said Thomas Telford.'

The life story

Along with the use of dialogue, this sort of biography will differ because it will follow much more of a narrative style. 'This is the story of the life of ...' Of necessity, the book will be much shorter than an adult biography, so you may need to select a portion of the life to focus on. The most obvious section is the famous part, or the moment when the subject made their big discovery. In this case you could even open with that scene immediately, making only cursory references to the subject's past.

Alternatively, you may choose to write a book about the childhood of a famous person so that the young reader is able to make a comparison with their own life as they read. You might choose this approach to complement another account covering the famous period in the subject's life. Or you may assume that the child's general knowledge makes them aware of the subject's claim to fame. Or your description may be designed to give as much a flavour of early nineteenth-century childhood as of Charles Darwin's young life.

Collected biographies

There is another option which really exists only in the children's market and that is a collection of brief biographies. You may have a particular knowledge or interest, say, in early sailors or inventors. It might be possible to choose six important people in the field and write a brief life story for each. It would not be possible to tell their whole story in so few words, but you could dramatize the most exciting moment of each life and base your brief biography around that. The skill would be in selecting the significant achievements and presenting them in an entertaining way.

Content

The length of the book and the way in which the topic is tackled are particular considerations for biographies written for children. Material you choose to include, and any you choose to leave out, will be dictated by the age of the child.

Details of the subject's sex life are an obvious area where the content will differ from one for an adult readership. If you feel that your subject's sexual proclivities cannot be left out of the biography or watered down because they are essential to an understanding of him or her, then I would question whether this was a good subject for the children's market in the first place.

It isn't just the sexual angle that needs special consideration in writing for children. There may be difficult philosophical or religious issues that may require some explanation and may test your writing skills to the limit.

It can be difficult to know just how much knowledge to take for granted and how much to explain without patronizing the child reader. If they think you are treating them like children then you are finished!

TRY THIS

■ Choose a subject for a biography that might interest a nine-year-old.

■ Which part of the life would you concentrate on?

■ Write a paragraph for that age group. If you are feeling brave, rewrite the same information with a thirteen-year-old in mind.

---

25 ORGANIZING AND WRITING UP YOUR FAMILY HISTORY

Organizing your material

It may be that the biography, or biographies, which you have been researching have actually been connected with your own family. Family history is a fascinating and fast-growing hobby falling somewhere between biography, autobiography and history. No matter how you categorize it, the chances are that you have amassed a wealth of information and wonder how on earth you can get it into some manageable form.

The writing-up process is going to be similar to preparing a biography, but with one crucial difference. The family history account is likely to include *most* of what is known about the family. By contrast, as a biographer, you would select *only* that material from your research which best supports your argument. Much of what you have discovered is not used directly. In some ways writing a family history is closer to writing a history book, because you are not so much setting out to construct an argument as trying to make sense of events and document them.

The timeline

The timeline you used for your research (see page 19) may actually be a valuable inclusion in this finished book. It will help the reader keep a grasp on international, national and local events at the same time as reading about how their great-great-grandfather lost his job at the brick kilns. It may also be possible to illustrate the timeline with little cameo pictures of some of the people at key times in their lives – use wedding or school photographs for example.

Where do you start writing?

With biography the answer was usually at the beginning. With family history you could start at either end. You could begin your account with the earliest members of the family you have researched and follow their story through to yourself and the present day and, perhaps, your descendants. However, it may well be easier to start with yourself and work backwards through the generations to the earliest forebears. Both ways are perfectly valid. The second method has the added merit of making it easier to absorb newly discovered material as you come across it. It is simply your own preference.

Who do you follow?

This is a perennial problem with researching family history because everybody is interesting. Added to that, you often find that you have discovered most material about somebody who was *not* part of your main strand of research. You have probably already solved this question during your research. You may have decided to tracked a surname backwards or you may have followed the lineage of a certain person. If that person was female, you have probably gone through a series of surnames.

When you plan the writing-up you have lots of options. These are just a few possibilities:

- You can construct each chapter around one generation, taking a key character but referring to the progress of his or her peers.
- You can take one strand of the family and follow them forward or backwards through the book, ignoring the siblings.
- It may be more appropriate to centre each chapter on a place and look at the family's activities in that area over the years.
- Or you could have a chapter for one surname and track that back and forth, although this may mean that you follow only the male line and lose the women in the family.

Who is going to read it?

This is not meant to be a rude question. When the subject is a family, there are usually loads of people itching to read what you have said and they will be as interested to learn, as you were, about past generations. So finding readers is unlikely to be difficult.

But you need to consider whether you intend to produce:

■ one copy of this family memoir – basically a record of your family to which you can continue adding material and hand down to future generations

■ numerous copies of this family history to give or sell to branches of the family – I say *sell*, not because you are undertaking a commercial activity in order to make a quick buck out of the relatives, but because you may well need to cover your costs (there are probably several family members very keen to read their family history and more than happy to assist in financing the enterprise)

■ a family history to inform the children of their heritage, in which case, you will need Chapter 24 about writing for children – bear in mind that it may be particularly difficult to write for *all* the children in the family because they are probably of widely varying ages, which makes it hard to pitch the language.

■ a volume to be housed in the local reference library or county archives – if you have produced a family history with strong links to an area, these public bodies will be grateful for a copy and will preserve it for posterity, (you will have done something worthwhile and you may gain knowledge if people make contact with you to add snippets of information or donate pictures).

What form will the book take?

The form may well be dictated by the readership and the costs. As with autobiography it is virtually impossible to find a commercial publisher prepared to undertake what is essentially a personal venture.

Your own record of the family

It is easier to think of the enterprise in this way. You will probably want to continue adding to the book and it is highly unlikely you will ever believe you have finished. There are always other strands you could have followed and dead ends you have not been able to unblock. And unlike biography research, your material continues to be generated with each passing day. New members of the family are born, existing ones die or achieve something noteworthy to add to the family saga. Because of this your final product might best appear in a ring binder (or two or three!) with sheets displayed in polythene wallets to stop them getting damaged. The advantage of the ring binder is that you can intersperse the illustrations between the written pages in the appropriate places. At any time and in any place you can add new information or pictures. The whole enterprise is cheap to set up, but still looks professional. If you decide you want another copy or two, you can replicate the folder by photocopying or printing more pages off the computer.

Copies for the main branches of the family

These can certainly be in folder form, but if you want to go to greater expense, then you might consider having a book printed. Costs can vary tremendously depending on how large the book is, the number of illustrations and how many copies you want. Nevertheless printing under 100 copies of any book is extremely costly. Read Chapter 30 for some guidance on self-publishing. A compromise might be to have some copies of the family history spiral-bound in a plastic or wire binder, which is a cheaper method.

Once the family history is produced in book form it is set in stone, so the interesting reminiscences, stories or photographs that come to light because your book jogged a few memories can't be included. You could produce a second edition, but this may not prove as easy as it first seemed. The new information that comes to light is likely to belong in all different sections. Someone may tell you of the existence of another child of great uncle Fred's; a birth date for somebody else and give you two superb photographs of granny's cottage in the wood. If this is likely to happen, a ring binder could prove the best solution.

Illustrations

Photos and portraits

These are even more necessary than in a biography. Your readers, predominantly family members, will long to know what their ancestors looked like and whether anyone has inherited their features. So include all the portraits you can lay your hands on. Saying that, the more recent you get, the more the photographs proliferate, so some selection of the subject at different ages may be necessary.

Similarly, most of the houses the family members lived in are of interest. Don't forget the ones they are living in today, because we hope your family history will be passed on in the family and added to over the years.

You probably want to include as many photographs as you can glean from the family archive, but the costs can escalate. Consider whether they could be photocopied or computer scanned then printed. Photographs do not actually have to feature family members, but could be of significant events they were involved in. For instance, you may have a picture of the Civil Rights march through Uncle George's town or a street party for the Coronation. They all belong to the family's past – the people may not feature because they actually took the photograph! Add an appropriate caption to link the photo to the family.

A family tree

In this book, a family tree is essential, whereas in other biographies it is optional. If you have managed to go back a long way in your family research, or have followed different strands of the family sideways, you may have lots of information to include. There are many ways of producing family trees from diagrams to lists. A huge fold-out family tree may not be practical. Not just because it is cumbersome, but creases and folds weaken over the years and there is a risk of sections becoming detached and getting lost.

Maps

These may be useful if the family lived in and around one area for a long time or if there was a family estate with extensive land. But if the different generations are dotted around the country, or even the world, maps may add little to the project except cost.

TRY THIS
- Construct the best arrangement for your family history.
- Work out the contents of each chapter.

26 | INTRODUCTIONS, ACKNOWLEDGEMENTS, REFERENCES AND PERMISSIONS

Do you need an introduction?

It is not vital to have an introduction, but it helps the reader get into the subject gently, rather than dropped straight in amongst the ancestors. Strangely, the introduction is best written *last*. You may have ideas for an introduction at the outset. Note them down, but put them to one side. Only when you get to the end can you see the whole life in perspective.

What goes into the introduction?

Whatever you like. This is your opportunity to talk to the reader yourself, outside of the life story. You do not really get another chance.

You might like to use the introduction to tell the reader what approach you are going to take, or why you became fascinated by the subject in the first place. This is also the place for the personal asides. The reader may well enjoy hearing that you grew up in one of the houses your subject lived in or that you once discovered a map by a cartographer which set you off on the trail of the man.

The introduction can be used to explain a point about the research. I was refused access to one particular set of family papers and I feared this might have compromised my final biography, so I said so. With my biography of four sisters, inevitably I developed a favourite. I thought it only fair to say that in the introduction and to give the reasons why.

An introduction can be very brief, only a few hundred words, but I think it is worth writing. To some extent you are introducing yourself, as well as the subject. As a reader, I am always interested in the author's anecdotes and attitude towards the subject. I enjoy being taken into the author's confidence and told what they thought of the subject – the high points and the exasperation.

As has been said before, your introduction will depend on who you envisage as your reader. Read different introductions and opening chapters in published biographies to decide what you think works and what fails.

Acknowledgements

It is likely there are many people and organizations who have helped you in the course of your research. This is the place to say thank you. The acknowledgements are likely to range from a formal thanks to the trustees of some national museum who permitted access to the papers, to a mention of the friend up the road who called in regularly to take the children off your hands, or agreed to go and take some photographs of a house whilst on holiday.

It can help to group the institutions together with introductory thanks and then an alphabetical list. This may be followed by another paragraph of people listed alphabetically who offered help with research. They may simply have answered a letter or sent you a photocopy of an old map but they do need thanking. They have probably given their time, and quite often hospitality too, for no monetary gain. When you list people try to be consistent with titling. If you decide to call a person Mr Albert Fornley rather than Albert Fornley, then title everyone.

The final paragraph of acknowledgements is usually the very personal thanks to the person who walked your dogs, did the typing or lived with you through all the traumas of researching and writing.

Say thank you to everybody, even if you do have to spend time trawling through your files collecting names off letters, notes and scraps. Everybody likes to see their name in print. It costs you nothing to say thank you and some of the people named in the book will buy copies of your book for themselves and as presents. Always worth bearing in mind!

References and notes

You need them and they will drive you up the wall to do. Quotations you have used in your text have to be fully acknowledged in terms of their source and you may need to request permission to publish them in your biography.

References from books

If the quotation came from a book, these details need to be listed:

- author
- title
- publisher (this can be optional)
- place of publication
- year
- page number.

At the point in the text where the quotation is used, give a number in brackets at the end of the sentence: 'Gladys was taken to watch operations from the age of five by her mother. (6)'

At the back of the book in the notes and references this quotation will be given as:

(6) Martin Armstrong, *The Life of Gladys Membury*, Simpson and Pearce, London, 1954 p62.

References from unpublished sources

References to unpublished sources, such as letters, are also incorporated into this system. A letter is listed like this:

- writer to recipient
- date
- source.

This might appear as:

Amos Fountain to Bill Membury, 19 January 1945, in the Shropshire County Record Office (SCRO).

If you subsequently refer to sources in the Shropshire County Record Office you would only need to put SCRO for the source. Always mention in full the first time, adding the abbreviation that you will be using subsequently in brackets.

Letters held in some archives may have been catalogued and, if so, will bear their own catalogue number. This needs to be quoted along with the source. For example:

Philip Beningham to Mary Drew, 18 Dec 1917, British Museum Add Mss 46246

References from periodicals

You may have used a quotation or some factual material from a journal or periodical. That too requires acknowledging and the following information is needed:

- magazine title
- volume number
- date
- page number.

For example:

Folklore Society Journal, No 84, 1947, p3–4.

As you are writing each chapter, keep the exact reference details close to the quotation. I actually keep them in the text, by putting them in brackets (often in my own abbreviated form) after the quote. I dread losing the reference for a quote. It takes ages to find the exact page of a book that sentence occurred on. Words like needle and haystack spring to mind!

Keying the references in

When you have finished each chapter, and polished it up into more or less its final form, extract the references from the text and replace them with a number. Initially, a specific list of references can go at the end of each chapter. Number sequentially within every chapter, rather than starting with one and going right through the book. The numbers can get very unwieldy by the end of chapter 20!

When the book is totally finished, you can collect up the references from the end of every chapter and group them at the back of the book, chapter by chapter. As a researcher, I have always found it helpful when all the information about a chapter (title, dates and number) is restated at the back, rather than simply referred to as Chapter 4 for example, because I tend to lose track of which chapter I was in.

In the past footnotes were a popular way of doing references but this method has largely been dropped in favour of the system I have described.

Adding notes

You may want to add a word of explanation about something you have written in the text but without interrupting the flow of the narrative. This can be done easily by adding a number in brackets at the end of the sentence in the text. Then develop the point in the Notes and References section at the back.

Ibid

Ibid is a useful word in lists of references. Use it when you are referring to another page in the same source as the one listed immediately above. For example:

5   M H Spielman & G S Layard, *The Life and Work of Kate Greenaway*, London, 1905 p73

6   Ibid p104

But if something breaks the sequence then you have to repeat the reference, at least in terms of the authors. If you are quoting from more than one book by Spielman and Layard, to avoid confusion you will have to restate the whole title.

Formatting references

Don't worry too much about getting the format of the notes and references absolutely correct. Most publishers have their own particular style of presentation and your editor will tidy them up to accord with the house style. It is far more important to ensure that everything is fully credited to its source and is accurately transcribed word for word, with identical punctuation. At this point, you will appreciate the care you took taking notes during research and checking meticulously every time you transferred that information. It is a pain, but doing it properly the first time can save hours of frustration later.

Do you need permission?

Published material

Technically you require permission to quote from *anything* which is *published* and still in *copyright* (this continues for 70 years after the end of the year in which the author died). In practice a 'fair dealing' scheme has grown up which accepts limited use of copyright material without written permission, provided the title and author of the source are acknowledged. The UK Society of Authors suggests the following:

- ■ no more than 400 words for a single prose quotation
- ■ no more than 800 words in total for a series of quotations from a single prose work, with no more than 300 in each individual quote
- ■ no more than 40 lines of a poem, provided it does not exceed a quarter of the whole work.

If, however, you are quoting from a work in an anthology, you must have permission for any quotations no matter how short. Song lyrics do not come under the 'fair dealing' agreement.

Unpublished material

Quotation from any unpublished material, such as that held in a public archive or from a batch of letters kept in someone's wardrobe, does need permission for the use of even the smallest amount. You need to write a letter to the owner of the material, or to the original publisher of the book that you are proposing to quote from. Tell them who you are, what the book you are writing is about and who is going to publish it. Then give the exact quotation and its source. State that you are asking for their written permission to use it.

Do you have to pay?

You may have to pay if you are intending to publish your biography. If it was written for private circulation or to be read aloud to a writers' circle, no permission is needed. The copyright owners are perfectly entitled to charge whatever fee they choose for its use, payable on publication. They may decide that, if you are going to make money from the venture, so will they. However, it may not be as bad as it sounds because many publishers and authors are delighted that their work is to be quoted and charge nothing.

Is it you or the publisher who pays? The answer will lie in the terms of your contract with the publisher, but it is quite probable that you are responsible for the fees. If you anticipate the need for a large number of permission fees, it might be worth bearing that in mind when contracts are negotiated. Ask if the publisher will pay or is prepared to share the costs.

Paraphase

Costs and permissions all vanish, of course, if you decide to paraphrase a piece of material. This can be as effective as the original if you simply turn the writing into indirect speech. So you could write: 'In a letter the Reverend Charles Canning told her that he would still …' This remains close to the original but is now copyright free.

27 | BIBLIOGRAPHY, APPENDICES AND INDEX

Bibliography

As ever, the careful noting of details at the research stage pays dividends. When your biography is finished you do need to credit all your sources, not just because this is fair, but because anyone else wanting to do further research might want to follow them up. So go back through all your files for the details of:

- published books and articles
- unpublished material.

Published books and articles

Books are listed like this:

Author surname, first name or initials (as it appeared on the book), title, publisher (place of publication in brackets), date of publication, the edition if you are using one that is not the first.

Du Maurier, Daphne (ed), *The Young George Du Maurier: A Selection of his Letters* 1860-67, Peter Davies (London), 1951

Articles are listed like this:

Author surname, first name or initials, title of article, title of journal, edition number, date of publication.

Colvin, Sir S, 'Some Personal Recollections', *Scribner's Magazine*, Vol 67, 1920

Unpublished material or manuscript sources

These are listed separately:

Institution, town and country (if not the one where your book is being published): title of the manuscript collection, catalogue number if appropriate:

Bodleian Library, Oxford: Letters of F G Stephens.

East Sussex Record Office, Lewes, Sussex: Minutes of the Rottingdean Parish Council.

Publishers have their own house style which may vary slightly but that is no problem. Your editor will arrange the material to suit their publications. The bibliography goes at the back of the book in front of the index.

The appendix

This may sound as though it is only applicable to a medical biography but it is not! An appendix (or appendices in the plural) is similar to the bit inside people, in that it is a piece tacked on and you can do without. Most biographers do not set out to include an appendix in their book at all, but occasionally come across a really interesting extra piece of information they want to publish. For instance your research into Isabella Beaton may have uncovered a completely new recipe for nettle soup that you want to include. An appendix at the back is the only way.

At other times the biographer may feel the subject's will or a contemporary newspaper report would make interesting reading, but would interrupt the narrative if it were included in the main text. Then an appendix is justified and helpful.

Indexing

A word of warning! Whatever you do, *don't* index your manuscript.

Now this might seem a strange way to begin a section on indexing but if you index your manuscript you will have wasted your time and you will have to do the whole job again later. Indexing can't be done until the biography has reached page-proof stage. The words must occur in precisely the spot they will appear on the final printed page. If you are producing your own edition of the biography, the layout of your pages may well remain the same throughout (though it may not if you take it to a printer who typesets it for you). If you submit your manuscript to a publisher, it will be typeset in a different font on to a different-sized page and words will turn up in completely different places. Added to this, books have a knack of starting on weird page numbers like 5 or 7, rather than 1 as you might expect.

The professional indexer

Indexing is a highly skilled and professional job and whilst you can produce your own, it is unlikely to be as good as that provided by a professional. If you want to employ a professional indexer, they advertise in writers' magazines or you could contact the Society of Indexers for their list. Your publisher may be happy to commission an index for you although, depending on the details of your contract, you may have to cover the cost.

The DIY index

Once you have the pages fixed, that is you have reached page proof stage, or if it's your own publication and you have the final version as you want it, then you are ready to start.

It is possible to buy computer programs to index your book but a computer does not have a brain; it only does what you tell it. These programs may do an excellent alphabetical sort for you, but are not so good at deciding which are the important references and which are not. It is irritating, when you are researching, to look up a page reference that was in the index to find that the word is there, but adds absolutely nothing to your knowledge. I always imagine an index like this has been generated by a machine that simply flagged up every mention of the word but that couldn't check out the usefulness of each reference.

Opinions vary on how effective the index is if it is compiled by the author. I tend to think that the person who has written the book has the best knowledge of the contents, and consequently knows which references are helpful and which are not. Others may argue that the author is too close to the text and, as a result, does not know how the reader will approach the book or what sort of things they will want to look up.

If you are determined to index yourself, you need to get the kit: a highlighter pen, a tabulated notebook (like an address book) and an ordinary pen. There is an excellent *Quick Guide to Indexing Your*

Book published by The Society of Authors which can be purchased by non-members. Below are a few simple tips to start you thinking.

1 Go through the text with your highlighter and mark up every word or reference that you think needs to be indexed.

2 Take your tabulated book and work back through the text noting the word and page number against it: e.g. Barnstable 21, 63, 64, 71,116. It is useful to leave a line or two between entries, even more if you know this is going to be a popular one. Don't worry at this stage that the entries are not in alphabetical order within each letter category, just concentrate on spotting all the entries and putting them on the relevant page of your notebook.

3 Your subject – hero/heroine – involves more work because they probably appear on most pages. This category requires breaking down further into areas like birth; early life in Scotland; schooling; friendship with George II; university. How many categories you have is entirely up to you. Your aim is to help a reader get to the material they are seeking as quickly and painlessly as possible. The type of biography and the nature of the reader you envisage will dictate how detailed the index is. Another factor that dictates things will be the publisher who may say that you have got two pages with two columns for your index.

4 Once you have entered the whole text into your tabulated notebook, it is just a matter of arranging the relevant page into alphabetical order and typing it correctly.

5 Rationalize your numbers at this stage so Barnstable now appears 21, 63-4, 71,116

6 Names like *The Times* are usually best listed under the second word rather than the definite article eg *Times, The*. Do check names, they can catch you out so easily. Is it *The Independent* or the *Independent*?

7 Married names and maiden names need thought. Decide which is the most likely place for a reader to look and put all the page numbers there. Include other versions of the name and refer the reader to the one you have used.

Allingham, Helen (née Paterson) 14, 53, 74, 206

Paterson, Helen see Allingham, Helen

And when you think you have got your index finished, check every single reference. It is amazing how some numbers have changed themselves when you were looking the other way.

28 | HOW DO YOU END A BIOGRAPHY?

Possible endings

Death

One obvious answer to the question 'How do you end a biography?' might be the same way as life ends, with the death of the subject. If you have chosen to follow your subject through their life chronologically, as many biographers do, then you will arrive at the end. But you may feel that you have sold your reader and your subject short by just stopping.

And the hereafter!

This is not meant to be as metaphysical or as spooky as it might sound – death may not be the end of the story. For one thing the reputation of your subject did not end there, although it may have suffered a sharp decline at that point. There could be a case for writing some sort of epilogue in which you consider:

■ your subject's reputation in the short term
■ their contribution to the wider scene.

If neither of these categories is particularly appropriate, and certainly does not warrant a full chapter, then covering them in a paragraph or two might be a useful way of finishing the book. It is likely that, if the subject has sufficient standing to justify your biography, then some comment on their importance in the local, national or international stage is a good way to sum up.

Top and tail

It might be sensible to reread what you said in the introduction (or what you plan to say). Use your conclusion to pull together themes from your introduction. I admire the well-crafted book, fiction or non-fiction, where the author has carefully rounded it all off smoothly. It is very satisfying as a reader to see the opening neatly mirror the end. It gives the reader confidence in the author because everything appears under control. It gives the impression that the biographer has researched and understood fully. If only that were true!

In Chapter 26 about writing an introduction, I suggested that writing this at the outset can be hard and may well be what you do last of all. If you do this, you can construct the introduction in conjunction with the end of the book. This is especially useful if you decide to let the reader into your confidence and tell them what sort of preconceptions you had about the subject at the outset. If, in the introduction you offered some questions, make sure clear answers have been given by the end of the book.

I began my research into the life of Kate Greenaway with a question in mind. Why did she spend her life painting nursery scenes and never progress to anything else? Would she turn out to be a Peter Pan figure? Initially, I planned to open the book with these thoughts, lead the reader along the research trail with me, then at the end of the book, consider how far that idea was correct. However, it turned out that my initial hunch was spot on and, in fact, it was more useful to end the book looking at the fall and rise of her reputation after her death right up to the present day.

The descendants

In some biographies it can make a good ending to look at the paths that the descendants took and to see how much their lives were shaped by their famous forebear. On the other hand, you may feel uncomfortable ending the book with somebody other than the subject who has held centre stage throughout. You could title this section Epilogue and not give it a chapter number. In this way the subject remains the focus and this material becomes an interesting appendix.

When I wrote my biography of the four Macdonald sisters, of whom two were famous wives and two were famous mothers, their legacy was extremely relevant: Stanley Baldwin and Rudyard Kipling were more famous than their parents. But I also felt the reader would want to know if fame was in the genes. Did such interesting families continue to produce outstanding progeny? In that case an epilogue covering the fate of the descendants seemed natural.

The final sentence

It is hard to write the final sentence, not because you want to carry on writing, but rather because you feel you should leave the reader with some impressive thought to ponder during the rest of the day at least. The temptation is to write something incredibly pompous and high-minded, ruining all that has gone before. So avoid a great blast from the final trumpet. A better way to end the book might be with a short quotation from a contemporary or from the subject themselves. Perhaps choose something in which they say how they would like to be remembered or what they hoped for from their work.

TRY THIS

■ Plan two different final chapters you could use for a biography of Abraham Lincoln.

■ Would you have a different ending for a certain sort of reader?

Part Three –
PUBLICATION

29 | TO PUBLISH OR NOT TO PUBLISH?

What are the options?

For pleasure

There is enormous pleasure in just researching and also purely in writing. You don't necessarily need an audience. It is often assumed that everyone is desperate to see their work in print, but that is not true.

If you want to have an audience, it can be family and friends of your choosing. This is especially appropriate for autobiography or family history writings. Not only are these writings of particular interest to this group of readers (or listeners) but, conversely, the writings probably hold little interest for those with no personal knowledge of the main characters.

For others

Reading your work aloud to a select group, in a writers' circle for example, can also be great fun. The group know you and they can appreciate the trials and tribulations you have been through to produce your piece. They will give you immediate feedback, both as potential readers and as writers. Their suggestions can be extremely useful to the professional and amateur alike.

For posterity

Unpublished biography will not necessarily have a limited life like a piece of fiction might. Biography, autobiography and family histories have value to other researchers and interest groups. Consider placing a copy of your work in a local or county reference library or in archives in the area where the subject lived. Here your work will be preserved and be available to others for research purposes.

If you produce copies of your work for distribution amongst your family and friends, some of these are also likely to be kept, treasured and handed on. The only problem here is that the work will not enjoy the same acid-free special conditions of preservation it would in a public record office.

To publish

So you have chosen the proverbial *publish and be damned* route. Once again various choices present themselves. It important to bear in mind that this stage can take just as long as the researching and writing (or even longer), cost as much but, worse, may have no end product.

So after all the official health warnings are you still determined to have a go? Where do you start? The assumptions are that biographical writing has to be in book form. Well it doesn't and you may find that you stand more of a chance of getting published in a magazine.

The magazine article

Biographies do not have to be book length. Your research and writing up may have led to a neat vignette of 1000–1500 words. Or you may have decided to divide the life into three parts – childhood, early life and maturity – to produce a serial.

Once you settle on the idea of a magazine article, you will need to find a home for it. It is better to consider the destination for your article(s) before you begin writing because this will have a great bearing on the length and style of your piece. The feature article on the life of the great scientist that appears in a children's comic, Sunday colour supplement and scientific journal may be about the same person but will be vastly different in all other respects.

Remember the magazine market varies from the local to the international level and all possibilities are worth considering.

Community magazine

At local level there is the possibility of writing your material up for publication in the parish or community magazine. They might welcome a short description (probably around 500–750 words) of a local subject. They may be happy to receive a serialized version of the life. Payment is never an issue! This sort of magazine runs on a shoe-string but writing articles for it, pieces which are published and read, can be an excellent opening for a biographer. It is not something to look down your nose at. Plenty of professional writers contribute pieces to their village mag!

Local newspaper

The local weekly newspaper might accept an article about a local hero or heroine. If you think it is likely, write to the editor and propose it. Or you might consider sending in your article (with a self-addressed envelope to ensure its return). First, study the paper carefully and look at the type of feature articles which appear. How many words? Are they divided into short units with headings? What is the style? What percentage of the article is specifically local?

County magazines might also welcome an article on the life of a local personality.

Specialist magazine

There are numerous other magazines worth considering, many of which you never see displayed in the newsagents. Further research is needed here. You may be aware of the existence of some of these specialist publications through your own research – the watercolour journal that you consulted for the listings of your artist or a midwifery journal where you read about the pioneering use of a particular drug.

Large reference libraries, listings in catalogues and bibliographies and the Internet may all yield useful names and addresses. Study some of these publications to see whether there is one which might take your article. Remember that, though a journal may deal with on-going developments in the construction industry, they are always looking for something fresh to put in their publication. Your feature about a famous construction engineer in Victorian times may just fill that niche this month, especially if you have taken care to link it into present-day developments. Unlike the parish magazine, these glossy journals do have money to pay you.

And what about magazines that have a wide general interest circulation, like the ones tucked in the pocket on an aeroplane or left in the rack on the train for passengers to pick up? These expensively produced glossy magazines are always on the look out for general interest features. Could your life of the early woman pioneer be tailored to fit this sort of publication?

It is a case of experimenting to see whether you can cut your material to suit their needs: they are not going to come looking for you, that's for sure. Think about what sort of angle or slant you can put on the life story to make it ideally suited for their readers.

National and international magazines and newspapers

This area also requires a considerable amount of research if you are not to waste your time and money. Once you have located a magazine that you think might receive your article, you will need to read several back copies to be sure you have understood the type of material they publish and their readership. Reading copies of the magazines in the library saves money.

Newspapers also carry feature articles, especially at weekends. Can you find a topical slant to your biographical subject to interest them? Is there an anniversary coming up; a place that is in the news a lot at present, something which ties in with the subject or a seasonal connection you could exploit? Most important magazines commission their articles at least six months ahead of publication, so no matter how brilliant your article on Christopher Marlowe's childhood, if the anniversary of his birth is next week, you have probably missed the boat this year.

If your material is obviously too long for a magazine or newspaper article then publication in book form is the option to go for. But before you automatically dismiss the magazine market, consider whether you could sell your work in *both* areas. Since you have done all the research *and* written a book on the subject, surely you can manage a 1000 word article. Publishing a magazine article may well generate interest – whet the appetite – for a future biography.

TRY THIS

■ Which magazine do you think might be interested in a biographical article about Lord Byron or Ruby Wax?

■ Choose a subject whose life story might appeal to your own county magazine.

30 BIOGRAPHY PUBLISHING – THE DIY METHOD

What if no publisher wants you?

I have written at some length about a commercial publisher producing your biography, but sometimes it proves almost impossible to get published that way. You may consider doing it yourself. You have two main options here: either you pay someone to publish it for you or you publish it yourself.

Vanity publishing

This is hardly a pleasant sounding course of action and rather suggests an association with the Seven Deadly Sins than your manuscript! Whilst it is widely known as vanity publishing in the UK, or private printing in the US, those working in this market prefer the name *subsidy publishing*. And you can guess who might be subsidising whom! I think even subsidy publishing is a misnomer because you are doing more than part-paying for the publication, you are footing the whole bill, including *their* profit margin.

Vanity publishers advertise in many magazines and weekend newspapers. You have probably noticed their small adverts saying things like 'Publisher looking for authors', 'Does your book deserve publication?' or other similar enticing words. If you respond, they will probably invite you to send your manuscript in to be read. Fairly promptly you will receive a glowing report on it, indicating that, although they do not accept everything that is sent to them, your book definitely merits publication. The suggested costs are also enclosed.

Read the small print!

I hasten to add that not all vanity publishers are sharks. It would be unfair to say that. They are offering a service that some people want and are happy to pay for. What they do offer is an easy – though not cheap – way of turning your manuscript into copies of bound books. They are usually *not* offering anything else. In essence they are printers. Advertising, marketing and distribution to bookshops are your concern.

As with every contract, the small print needs enlarging! Horror stories abound of writers who have paid several thousand pounds to have their book published, only to land up with 100 copies when they thought they were going to receive 2000. It is not that the vanity publishers have ripped them off, rather that they did not read the contract carefully enough. What they might have paid for was a print-run of 2000 with copies being supplied 100 at a time. That sounds useful, especially when you consider your spare room, or lack of it, being piled high with books. What the unsuspecting writer may not have noticed was that when he or she applies for the next batch of a 100 books, there is a binding fee payable. If you don't want to pay that fee you may well be able to collect what you have already paid for (or pay a storage fee for the publisher to retain the sheets). But are 1900 printed, uncut, unfolded, uncollated and unbound sheets going to be any use?

Some vanity publishers offer to send out review copies of your books. Ask a few questions before you pay anything for this service.

- Which magazines or journals are going to receive your book?
- Have you heard of these magazines or are they so obscure (or subscription only) that few people read them anyway?
- Are readers of such a magazine likely to be interested in this sort of biography?
- Is the magazine likely to accept your book for review? After all anyone can send them in, but that is no guarantee they will be reviewed. Journalists know the names of vanity publishers and rarely review their books.

Despite all those warnings you may decide vanity/subsidy publishing is for you. Using someone to turn your biography from manuscript to finished copy does take the headache out of it and, when you have read the terms carefully, you may decide this is a service worth purchasing. Many people do: there are a number of vanity publishers and they do survive.

The real DIY solution

With time, lots of energy and money you could decide to print and publish the biography yourself. There is much fun to be had, you have total control over the project and, if there's any money to be made out of it, it will be yours.

Costs

Costing a biography is like measuring the proverbial piece of string. Authors producing a professional-looking paperback biography with a colour cover but no illustrations have found themselves relieved of a few thousand pounds. However, there are lots of variables involved, so that figure should not be regarded as definitive.

It is worth thinking of the book production in two parts:

     1 getting the text on to film
     2 printing and binding.

The editor

Once you have got your text as polished as possible you might consider paying for the services of a professional editor. An editor has usually worked in commercial publishing as a full-time employee but gone freelance. They often continue to take in work from commercial publishers and from others. Not surprisingly, they have a good insight into the market and valuable expertise to bring to your text. Names and addresses of such editors appear in writers' magazines and literary magazines. They will charge you a fee for reading and shaping up your manuscript so that it is ready on disk for publishing.

Graphic design

Again not vital, but if you want the words to look good on the page, this might be money well spent. The graphic designer will work on the format of the book – things like typeface; page layout; chapter beginnings; whether there are running headings and where the page numbers appear. These are things we often take for granted, but actually make all the difference to the look of the book.

The designer can also devise a concept for the book jacket. It is worth having an idea what sort of image you want to use. Traditionally, biographies have a portrait of the subject on the cover and this may be particularly advantageous if you cannot afford to put illustrations inside. Indeed, you might consider a collage of several portraits of the subject at different stages of their life, forming the front cover or even wrapping around to the back of the book. Colour covers cost more than using a single colour. So it might be possible to hold the costs down by going for a black-and-white cover, which would suit the black and white photographs nicely. A sepia-coloured cover on cream paper but has the added advantage of appearing old. If the pictures you propose using on the jacket are not your property, you will need to budget for the cost of loaning and reproducing them. Having a laminated cover on a soft back book makes it last longer and looks better. It also costs extra.

You don't have to have a photograph on the cover. Pieces of artwork could be used, such as cartoons, sketches or paintings, although this is less common with biography. For the cheapest option, have no picture at all, simply use the title in a decorative font.

The DTP Package

You can duck out of paying anyone to do these earlier stages and do the work yourself. There are an ever-increasing number of Desk Top Publishing programs on the market which, with a moderate amount of IT literacy, or the help of an evening class, you could master. You would need to shop around carefully to select the package best suited to your needs and abilities.

Using a DTP program, you could not only put your text on disk but design the page layout with the pictures imported into the exact place you want them. You would then be in a position to supply the disk to the printer. It is *vital* that you talk to a printer before proceeding down this route. They will be able to give you very specific instructions about the best way to supply them with your material. It would be devastating to lay out your entire book only to find that the printer cannot access your computer files.

The printer

This is an area where it is vital to phone or write around for costings. They can vary enormously depending on things like the printer's specialism; the quality of the paper; the print run and perhaps how much they want your business.

Besides the standard bound book format, the printer might be able to offer a much cheaper spiral binding if the book is thick and the print run small. Along with a colour photocopy cover under an acetate sheet, you could have a less expensive but professional-looking edition. This would be especially appropriate for the family history or autobiography. This type of binding service is also available through the many high street outlets specializing in photocopying and so on.

A book that is being published, rather than just privately distributed, and which you hope to sell to bookshops, will need that bar code on the back. The International Standard Book Number (ISBN) enables the book to be identified and ordered all round the world. The printer can usually assist you to get the ISBN, which is supplied on a small piece of film. I recommend that you do not print a price on the cover for the reasons which follow.

Distribution

With the private printing of family memoirs, distribution is not a problem. You have probably got them queuing up for their copies – possibly some proffering money to assist with production costs. But for biographies of other people you are going to have to work hard (as if you had not done enough already!) to get them into the market place.

There are firms which specialize in distributing books for independent publishers and you might consider approaching them to take on yours. They usually work on a percentage basis and you could expect the bookseller and distributor combined to take 55% of your retail price.

The advantage of using a distribution company is that their sales representatives will take your book around the country, wherever it is that you are based. They will probably get to many more shops than you could realistically get around, assuming the bookshops would grant you an audience. On the downside, their average selling time is 30 seconds per title, so your biography has got to hit the bookseller between the eyes first time.

If you decide to organize your own distribution locally – and you can still do that in addition to what any distribution company might do – then you will need to visit all your local bookshops. It does not have to be just bookshops either. Are there any Tourist Information Centres, gift shops, village shops, newsagents (in fact absolutely any outlets) that might be persuaded to take copies? Don't be surprised if they will only have them on a sale or return basis, this is quite normal. Be clear before you start exactly what discounts you are offering. Shops expect anything between 33% and 50%. For this reason you would be well advised not to put a price on the cover of the book when you have it printed. This enables you and others to set the retail price that is appropriate at the time. Look around at the retail price of similar books as a guide to what you could charge.

Marketing your biography

1 You could write an article for a magazine or newspaper (see page 140). This is a good way of generating interest in the subject. Then include your address, which is likely to be your home or a PO box number, where copies can be obtained. Decide on your copy price, plus how much a jiffy bag costs and the cost of postage. Do you want to add on a small amount for your time in preparing copies to post? Along with the cost of the book by mail order, be sure to state who cheques should be made out to.

2 Place a small advert in a magazine. Weigh up the cost involved in advertising a mail order service in an appropriate magazine. This could generate reasonable sales.

3 Letters, even flyers, could be sent to special interest groups offering mail order copies. You might consider special incentives or offers to groups like this; perhaps a discount for orders of 10 or more copies.

4 Talks are good for selling books. There are lots of groups permanently on the look-out for speakers for

their meetings: WIs, dinner clubs, literary organizations, all sorts. I am constantly amazed at the different societies I get invitations from. Yes, they do pay a fee and travel. It may be modest in the case of a local WI, but I enjoy going and I am not out of pocket. I do usually sell a few copies at the time and often get requests ages later from someone who heard me speak and suddenly thought my biography would do nicely for a friend's birthday present. You can write to groups who use speakers (ask the local library for names) and offer your services with an indication of fee. I would advise not being too greedy about the fee – what you really want is a captive audience for your talk. If they like what they hear, your name will get passed round to other groups and you might even get a request for a return visit.

5 Author's fairs are another possibility. There are not many of them and they do charge a fee for your pitch. On the plus side they bring people in through the gate who have come to buy books. I have never made a fortune at such events, but I have sold books, met lots of other writers, and spent a good part of my earnings buying their books. But had a great time.

6 Don't be afraid to get out and tell people about your book. The local newspaper will be only too delighted to come and interview you and write a feature. It will cost you nothing, but will be good advertising. It is also worth telling local radio about your new biography.

7 A final point: remember to send free copies of your biography to national libraries and possibly others.

31 | GETTING YOUR MANUSCRIPT READY FOR PUBLICATION

Editing your own work

This is a polite word for correcting, revising and generally polishing up. Some writers assume that it's the publisher's job to do this, but that is a mistake. They will edit the manuscript, but I think you should polish and polish that manuscript to the best of your ability first. There is a matter of personal pride in what you can produce. I would hate anybody to think my spelling and punctuation are appalling, that I cannot organize my material or that my expression is naff. I purport to be a writer. If that is my craft then I should be able to do it reasonably well.

Apart from that, I will offer the best I can to a publisher because I want them to think favourably of me, and hopefully offer or accept more work in the future.

What should you look for?

Spelling and punctuation

After you have written the first draft of a chapter, go over it a few times to eliminate the obvious errors of spelling and punctuation. We all make them. Sometimes they are just slips, other times they occur because you genuinely could not remember how to spell the word. Computer spell checks are helpful, especially for typing errors you have not spotted, but spell-checkers are by no means fool-proof. They will recognize words spelt wrongly, but they will not pick up the wrong word spelt correctly: *there* and *their*, for example.

Organization

Another thing to look for when you reread your work is the organization of the material. Whilst you planned your chapters very carefully at the start and worked to that plan, as the material has unfolded, or your thinking has developed during the writing, some information may need reordering. Don't be afraid to do it. The chapter plan you made at the outset was to help you not constrain you. What matters most is how it works in practice. It is often easier to consider the organization of the chapter at a later date. When it is freshly written, you are often too close to it. Two days later, even two weeks or better still two months later when you can reread a chapter in the context of the chapters on either side, you will know straightaway whether it flows well or whether there is something wrong with the organization of the material.

Explanations

Another thing to check is whether you have given sufficient explanations. Do you, for instance, refer to something by initials, which you have never introduced to the reader? If so, you need to weigh up whether the reader you have in mind could reasonably be expected to understand or whether they will need a word of explanation. It can be a difficult balancing act between informing and insulting their intelligence. But, if in doubt, explain the term.

Repetition

This is one of my great failings. Either I have mentioned something twice in different ways during the course of the chapter or I put down that same information in an earlier chapter I wrote months ago and forgot about. Just checking a single chapter alone will not throw that up, but when you have finished and read the whole book through sequentially, it should jump out at you. Similarly, you may find on re-reading that you have used the same word or phrase twice within a few lines. Change one of them.

Expression

Polishing up the expressions is one of the most enjoyable bits of editing because it makes you feel like a *real* writer. You may read through a passage and suddenly get a flash of insight as to how you could say the same thing in a better way or could put it more succinctly. You might come up with a clever play on words or a carefully balanced turn of phrase. Once again this sort of polishing becomes easier the more time has elapsed between writing and checking. When the text is extremely fresh you read only what you intended to say, not what is on the page, and you frequently anticipate the words because they are still in your mind. With a reasonable space of time you can come to the chapter as a new reader would, admiring the good bits and wincing at the rough bits.

Try reading the text aloud to yourself. This can be a brilliant way of discovering the parts that do not work because you stumble over them. It is strange how using your voice and ears, instead of your eyes, sharpens up the brain. It works. Sometimes you read and read a section, fiddle around with it for ages and still cannot get it right. A tip someone once gave me was to try striking it out completely. I hate doing it, but when I finally pluck up the courage to put a line through the whole sentence or paragraph, it usually solves the problem.

Try another reader

If you dare, let someone else read your work for you. They don't need to be an expert in any special sphere, just another pair of eyes. For one thing they will read what is on the page and not what is in your head. This is extremely useful and very hard for the author to do. They will spot the missing words, the duplications and query things they do not understand which will enable you to explain them better.

Almost anyone will do, a friend or partner, provided you trust their opinion. I freely admit that I never send out any work that has not been read and edited by my husband. I write a chapter, go over it myself then pass it over for him to look at. He is briefed in all the five key areas mentioned above! Then I get it back and go over his suggestions, put in corrections and have another go sorting out the bits he thought were muddled. The redraft may go back to him again then, particularly if I have made lots of changes. Or I may put the redraft aside and push on with the next chapter. When the whole book or article is finished I, and then he, will go through the whole text again, chapter by chapter in the order a reader would. I still find parts that I could express in a better way.

When do you stop polishing?

This is a hard thing to decide because you always feel that you could just improve on it a little bit more. I don't think there ever comes a time when you think your work is perfect, or even very good. But try to reach a point when you can say realistically that you have done the best you can, then stop. There is always a danger that you will over-polish the silver and begin to take the lovely patina off. Be reassured that what you submit is probably not the final version anyway. A copy editor will have a go at it for you, then the text will return to you and you can still make a few changes if you are convinced they are necessary.

Type it up

Does a manuscript have to be typed? Yes, without exception. No publisher will look at a manuscript that is handwritten. Fortunately the job of typing a book has become less arduous over the years, thanks to the advent of computers and word-processing programs. Many biographers will have been typing their work up as they go. Not everybody composes straight on to the screen. You do whatever you are comfortable with – the pencil, the fountain pen, even the quill if it inspires your best writing – then type the text up yourself or ask someone else to.

Layout

There is lots of fancy advice about exactly how many centimetres the margins should be and what the headers and footers should be. People in writers' circles often get unnecessarily paranoid about the exact specifications a publisher wants and believe no one will look at a manuscript that is not perfectly correct. No, it is far simpler than that:

1 Type on one side of the paper only.
2 If possible, no errors or corrections on a page. I would rather retype a page than send in one with a correction on, but that is not essential. I admit the odd correction is acceptable. I just think a clean copy creates a better impression.

3 Double spacing is required. *Never* send in single spaced work. It looks far too cramped and leaves no space for editorial changes to be written between the lines.

4 Never justify the right-hand margin.

5 Leave a margin of at least 40mm or 1" all round the page, again for the editor.

6 Number the pages (think of the person who drops the manuscript on the way to the photocopier).

7 Don't have it bound or stapled, again for photocopying purposes.

Don't Desk Top Publish it!

Unless your biography is a self-publishing venture and you are intending to supply the printer with a disk of the page layout, do not attempt to design the pages for the publisher. Few publishers will thank you for that. Most likely they will curse you because it takes them ages to *unpick* it ready for a professional designer to get to work.

TRY THIS

■ Take a page of something you have written recently and polish it up looking out for the five areas mentioned in this chapter.

■ Reread it a week later and see if there are any further improvements you would make. Try reading it out aloud this time.

---

32 | KNOW YOUR MARKET

Who is waiting to receive your manuscript?

We all hope the whole world is waiting for our masterpiece, but sadly that is not usually the case. Finding a home for your biography can be difficult and may take a long time. Although this chapter appears towards the end of the book, the thought needs to be at the back of your mind from the outset. Much has been said about the reader and their expectations of the biography (see page 61) but the publisher also needs to be considered because you need someone to buy your product and to want to publish it.

Choosing a publisher

There are various places to find the names and addresses of publishers, but you want to avoid wasting your own and their time by contacting the wrong ones.

Go to a bookshop

What you need to know is who is currently publishing the sort of book you have written. Your first port of call is a large bookshop. Look for hardbacks on the shelves of the biography section. Hardbacks are your most useful source of information because most biographies come out in hardback first, followed by a paperback edition perhaps six months later. So by all means look at the paperback editions afterwards, but remember that the paperback publisher probably bought the rights from the original hardback publisher.

Whichever book you pick up, turn to the copyright page. It is always on the left-hand page near the front. If you look at this book, you will find it comes immediately after the title page. The copyright page carries quite a lot of publishing information about the volume, but you are interested in the name of the publisher. Sometimes more than one publisher's name is mentioned if the book began life elsewhere, then you are looking for the words 'first published by …' or role whichever publisher has the earlier publication date.

From the copyright page write down the address of the publisher. Collect as many suitable publishers' names and addresses as you can. It is worth checking the paperback editions to see where they began life and note that name and address too.

Should you go to the library?

After all your heavy use of the library for previous biographical research, this is probably one occasion when the libraries will not be so helpful to you. Their strength, from a research point of view, is that they hold lots of volumes that have been long out of print. Now that is the last thing you require!

A visit to a large city reference library will show you the range of books published on a similar topic and, if the library is not too strapped for cash, it may have been able to buy recent publications. From their catalogue, you may be able to identify books published within the last year or two (at the most – you do not want them any older) and note their publisher. A city library may have a greater selection of books on a specific subject than a bookshop, which aims to stock a little of everything. The library may score over the bookshop in shelving the work of very small independent publishers that never get a look-in at the big bookshop chains.

Looking for a publisher

The Writers' and Artists' Yearbook

Aspiring writers often believe it is vital to buy a copy of this *bible* every year in order to locate the right market for their work and I am sure the publishers of this particular book would wholeheartedly support this view. The book is useful to check out names and addresses of publishers you located in the bookshop or library but on its own it is only of limited use in finding the right publisher. The book does, however, have lots of other useful articles in it. The danger with just using a list of publishers and the type of information given with each entry is that you only get a tiny part of the story. Sending your manuscript to someone who lists biography amongst their output may be courting failure, unless you have seen a copy of one of their biographies. If they produced a glossy, heavily illustrated paperback about the winner of last year's US Open, it is unlikely they would accept your well-researched biography of Disraeli.

If you are not sure whether the publisher you have located is likely to welcome your type of book, you can always write to them asking for their current catalogue.

The Book Clubs

Whilst you certainly should not waste your time posting your manuscript to a book club – they are not publishers merely mail order bookshops – they might be useful to you. There are various specialist book clubs offering books on gardening, warfare or history, to quote but a few. Scrutinize the catalogue of one offering topics akin to your biography to see if you can identify potential publishers. This needs care. The publisher who produces cookery books probably does not want your biography of Mrs Beeton, but amongst the recipe books the Cookery Book Club may occasionally offer related topics. You could see who publishes these titles.

Do you look abroad for a publisher?

The general advice would be not to look for a publisher outside your country of residence, but there could be exceptions. If you have written a biography of a person who was a great hero in another English-speaking country, there might be a case for approaching a publisher in that country. Locating a suitable publisher in another country could be difficult unless your research and travels have made you very familiar with that market. A foreign publisher may well wonder why the book is not being published in your own country first and those editions, or foreign rights, are not being offered subsequently. But nothing ventured nothing gained.

TRY THIS

■ Can you research four publishers who might be interested in an illustrated biography of Charlie Chaplin?

■ Look at a copy of *The Writers' and Artists' Yearbook* published by A & C Black or *The Writer's Handbook* published by The Writer Inc. to see the sort of information it offers.

33 SENDING YOUR WORK IN

Take your life in your hands

This is the dreaded moment of truth, you have written the book and you have compiled a list of at least six publishers you are now going to try your luck with.

Make that phone call

Ring the publisher up first and ask the person on the switchboard for the name of the commissioning editor for biography. This enables you to target them specifically with your work and might prevent the manuscript being put into the proverbial 'slush pile'.

The letter

The letter is best kept fairly short and straight-forward, so that your work can speak for itself. The main reason for the letter is to accompany your work, rather than to introduce yourself. Avoid beginning with a long rigmarole about who you are or the real turn-off: 'This is the first time I have ever written anything like this. If I haven't got it quite right please could you give me some tips about improving it …' and so on.

It might be best to launch straight into 'I enclose a proposal for a biography of …, who …' This would make a substantial paragraph.

Follow with reasons why you believe there is a market for this sort of biography. Here you could mention any forthcoming anniversaries or events that would link in with such a biography (at least 18 months ahead).

You might conclude with a brief statement about your own special interest or qualification for writing this book. Take care, a copious list of academic qualifications may not cut any ice, unless of course you are writing especially for the academic market. Where you do mention qualifications, try to show how appropriate they are to this particular task.

As well as avoiding being horribly humble and self-deprecating, do not go to the other extreme. The person who makes extortionate claims for their book and themselves is likely to weaken their case.

Some writers like to write to an editor first enquiring whether the editor would be interested in reading their manuscript. If they get the go-ahead, then they send in the whole script. Because I fear that method is too slow and I am an impatient person, I prefer to send a proposal for the book along with a specimen chapter – to whet the appetite. I also hope that I stand more chance of getting a favourable response if an editor has more to get their teeth into.

The proposal

This goes on a separate sheet from the letter and can take various forms, according to personal preference. It is likely to be three or four sides of A4 (around 1 000–1 500 words) and should:

- give an outline of the hero/heroine's life, indicating where the high points are
- explain your approach to this topic and why it is different from previous ones
- state your particular expertise
- comment on the market for your book
- list any strong selling points, such as it is based on new documents
- include a self-addressed envelope.

Alternatively you could send:

- a contents page
- a one page synopsis of the subject's life
- a specimen chapter, preferably one of your best from somewhere in the middle
- a photocopy of a couple of the best pictures with their captions, if you think that they are a good selling point
- a self-addressed envelope.

On no account send the whole manuscript to anyone, unless they ask to see it. And do not begin sending letters and proposals out until you have written the book. It is embarrassing to have to admit you have not written it, should you get the go-ahead to submit the manuscript. Embarrassment aside, the editor is not going to wait for you to write it. More likely, with the speed that editors change, the person you have been in touch with will have moved on and the new person may not be interested in their predecessor's ideas. Dashing something off because they are waiting to read it is unlikely to produce good prose. So only offer the manuscript if it really exists.

If the request for the rest of the manuscript comes, then send a paper copy in – no disks at this stage – and no original copies of pictures. If you do want to send any pictures (and there is no need yet, it is the *text* that is being considered) make sure they are photocopies.

What happens next?

Usually nothing happens for a long time, because the manuscript may go out to different readers for reports. This can easily take a couple of months which is no consolation to you, as you dash to the doormat every time the postman comes.

Under no circumstances ring the editor to see how things are going. After two months' silence you might write and enquire if any decision has been reached about your manuscript. A positive answer will not come bouncing back just because you dared to ask. You may just get your manuscript back in response to your enquiry – all you have done is to kick them into action to post it, rather than leave it languishing in a pile on the floor.

If this happens, choose the next editor's name and address on your list and begin the procedure again. If you have a plan for where to send your book next it helps to soften the blow of rejection a little.

Do not send out the same copy of the proposal that has just returned through the post, unless it honestly looks in mint condition. A tired creased copy that looks like it has been around a bit gives the game away and may not actually get read at all.

It is just a case of keep trying, one publisher at a time. There are always great controversies in writers' circles about whether it is ethical to shower everybody on your list with copies of your work simultaneously. Some say you should not, it is a matter of etiquette, rather like you not accepting lots of proposals of marriage at the same time! What would you do if everybody accepted?

Others argue that publishers show precious little respect or etiquette towards writers, keeping them waiting, losing their work or dumping them without a second thought, so it does not matter. I'll leave you to decide how you want to play that one. Publishers certainly play their cards close to their chest, to prevent others knowing what aces they hold. They are highly unlikely to discuss with each other whose work they are reading so you wouldn't get found out that way.

So go ahead and send your work on its way – wish it luck!

USEFUL ADDRESSES

Society of Authors, 84 Drayton Gardens, London, SW10 9SB. email: authorsoc@writers.org.uk

American Society of Journalists and Authors, 1501 Broadway, Suite 302, New York NY10036

Author's Guild, 330 West 42nd Street, 29th Floor, New York NY10036-6902

Society of Indexers, Globe Centre, Penistone Road, Sheffield S6 3AE

INDEX